Endorsement of *Tell Me*
By J. Robert Ewbank

Developing a popular, reader-friendly style, with personal narratives along the way, Robert Ewbank explores the organization, history and doctrine of the United Methodist Church in a very engaging manner. With a structure that is well suited for the task at hand, each chapter contains not only an opening Scripture, along with a suitable prayer, but also a number of probing questions that take the reader to a better understanding of the material. This is a very helpful book for those who would like to learn more about the largest mainline Protestant denomination in America today.
Kenneth J. Collins Ph.D.
Professor of Historical Theology and Wesley Studies
Director of the Wesleyan Studies Summer Seminar
Asbury Theological Seminary

Thanks for sharing with me your wonderful work, a great addition to the existing resources on Methodism. I appreciate your creative way of connecting history, beliefs, and polity with the membership or discipleship vows or commitment. I hope and pray that not only potential UM members or disciples but also existing members or disciples would greatly benefit from this book; in order to renew their commitment to the Methodist Movement. This valuable resource would intentionally turn local churches from their current reality to a better and brighter future with a greater commitment and fruitful ministry.
Superintendent Samuel J. Royappa
Capital Coulee Region/Districts
Wisconsin, Annual Conference, UMC

For New Comers and Old Timers alike, Bob Ewbank's *Tell Me About the United Methodist Church* provides an engaging, thoughtful, and comprehensive introduction, not only to the UMC but to Christian faith in general. By using the dialogical format of a new member's class, the readers are led to discover the rich heritage and profound beliefs of the church. Church doctrine is presented in a straight-forward fashion unbelabored by complex issues. Interspersed are scriptural guides for

spiritual reflection and review questions to solidify what is learned along the way. The book will be a welcomed resource by church leaders and laity across a wide spectrum of the church.
Richard N. Soulen, Ph.D
Professor of New Testament Studies, Virginia Union University School of Theology, Retired

This book is very readable, and will be very helpful to new believers "and old members", who are seeking to understand what we United Methodists believe. The lessons are presented in the setting of a group of people looking for an understanding of the United Methodist Church beliefs through a study of the Articles of Religion of the UMC. The material is presented in a way that does not lead to boredom and hence a loss of interest.

I am looking forward to the publication of the book and the study of it by our Sunday evening study group at New Market United Methodist Church.
Thomas Odom, layperson, New Market United Methodist Church

At a time when confusion abounds about the doctrines of the United Methodist Church, Robert Ewbank has provided a clear and accessible guide to the distinct structure and theology of our denomination that is nevertheless grounded in the ancient faith of the Christian Church. Newcomers and seasoned United Methodists alike will find this handbook informative and inspiring.
Rev. Matt O'Reilly
Pastor
St. Mark United Methodist Church
Mobile, Alabama

Thank you for the opportunity to read your book. It seems to me that the vast majority of new members in the Methodist Church are from other denominations or they have never been "affiliated with a denomination. It is important that they understand who we are, how we are organized and what we believe. Your book is an excellent tool for achieving all of the above.
It can also be very helpful as a refresher course for Individuals within the Methodist Church. Below are a few additional comments.

* All too often our new member classes consist of meet, greet, eat and get the new member/prospect signed up for a small group.
In fear of scaring them off, we shy away from telling them their role as a member of the Church. In my opinion, Chapter 10 is the key to the book, it answers the question, "What does the Church and God expect me to do?" ...

Earle King
BS from Univ of North AL, BS from Univ of AL and a MS in Management from Florida Institute of Technology.

Retired from CUMC in Dec 2006 as Church Administrator.(Christ United Methodist Church, Mobile, Alabama)

TELL ME ABOUT THE UNITED METHODIST CHURCH

An Introduction to the United Methodist Church

J. Robert Ewbank

TELL ME ABOUT THE UNITED METHODIST CHURCH

An Introduction to the United Methodist Church

Copyright © 2015 J. Robert Ewbank. All rights reserved. Except for brief quotations in critical publications or reviews, no part of this book may be reproduced in any manner without prior written permission from the author.

Because of the dynamic nature of the Internet, any web addresses or links contained in this book may have changed since publication and may no longer be valid. The views expressed in this work are solely those of the author and do not necessarily reflect the views of the publisher.

Printed by CreateSpace an Amazon Company.

Third Edition

ISBN: 13:978-1-514-72692-1

ISBN: 10-978-1-514-72692-0

Also by J. Robert Ewbank

John Wesley, Natural Man, and the Isms

Wesley's Wars (theological)

And

To Whom It May Concern

To my parents who taught me the value of education.

To my teachers who taught me to study and learn.

To my wife who put up with my work.

And

To The United Methodist Church.

Thank You

Contents

Preface		**xii**
Acknowledgements		**xiv**
Introduction		**xv**
Jim and Barb		**1**
Chapter 1	**Organization of the United Methodist Church** *Local Church, District*	8
Chapter 2	**Organization of the United Methodist Church (cont.)** *Annual Conference, Other Conferences Committees and Counsels*	25
Chapter 3	**History of the United Methodist Church** *Jewish Background, First Five Hundred Years, Protestant Reformation, John Wesley and Methodism*	36
Chapter 4	**Methodist Beliefs** *Holy Trinity, The Word (God and Humanity), Resurrection, Holy Ghost*	57
Chapter 5	**Methodist Beliefs (cont.)** *Original Sin*	77
Chapter 6	**Methodist Beliefs (cont.)** *Sufficiency of Scriptures for Salvation, Old Testament*	91
Chapter 7	**Methodist Beliefs (cont.)** *Justification, Sin after Justification, Sanctification (Christian Perfection)*	101

Chapter 8	**Methodist Beliefs (cont.)**	**118**
	Good Works, Works of Supererogation, Sacraments, Baptism, Lord's Supper, Both Kinds, One Oblation of Christ	
Chapter 9	**Methodist Beliefs (cont.)**	**138**
	The Church, Purgatory, Speaking in Tongues, Rites and Ceremonies	
Chapter 10	**What Must I do as a Member of the Church?**	**149**
	Prayers, Presence, Gifts, Service, Witness	
Study Answers		**168**
Bibliography		**186**

Preface

This book is a work of love for the United Methodist Church. I am the third in a line of Methodist Ministers.

My grandfather, John Robert Ewbank, while in England and later in the United States, worked as a coal miner during the week and then as a Methodist Minister on Sunday's and in all probability, at other times as well.

My father, John R. Ewbank was on the faculty at Philander Smith College in Little Rock, Arkansas and Westminster College, Salt Lake City, Utah.

I Graduated from Garrett-Evangelical in Evanston, Illinois and was in the full time ministry for ten years in the Methodist Church. Returned to Garrett three years later to work on a Master's in the theology of John Wesley which was completed with the exception of the thesis which was written but not finished and became my first book, "John Wesley, Natural Man, and the Isms."

I have argued with the Church at times (haven't most of us) but have always loved it and most often saw the wisdom of the Church.

This book is written to be a help in membership training, both as in Membership Training Classes themselves as well as being a useful training and educational tool for those who are already in the church, so they can better understand it and our doctrines. Though written for the United Methodist Church and Wesleyan churches, it is easily adaptable to others.

I read recently that our church in the long past was composed of people who came to the church through the classes and thus were well versed in Methodism. Today, many of the folks who have been "Methodists" for years are only vaguely aware of our past, our beliefs, and the other uniqueness's of Methodism.

It is my fondest hope that my efforts will be of help to ministers as they try to educate their congregations on this great church of ours.

The St. Mark of this book is not necessarily the St. Mark in the Mobile District where I attend. The characters in this book do not have anything to do with the real St. Mark church.

Acknowledgements

All books written are not created in a vacuum. They would not exist if it were not for the help and encouragement of many others.

My parents played a huge part in their encouragement of my many activities throughout my life. John R. Ewbank was a second generation Methodist Minister and college professor. Mattie Cook Ewbank was a teacher and profound helper and guide to me in my young and later life.

It is impossible for one to succeed in writing without some teachers they met along the way who have been a source of encouragement and mentoring. Although there were some in my earlier years those who particularly played a part in this creation came from Garrett Evangelical Theological Seminary, Evanston, Illinois.

Dr. William Hordern taught me to love the study of theology and Dr. Colin Williams taught and inspired me to love the theology of John Wesley. Special thanks must go to Dr. Philip S. Watson, counselor without peer, who worked with me on the theology of John Wesley when I returned to Garrett after graduating with my M.Div., and was seeking a Masters in the theology of John Wesley. It is with deep regret I was unable to finish the program.

Hanes Swingle, M.D., Pediatric Development and Behavior; Director, Autism Diagnostic Clinic; Professor, Pediatrics graciously let me use one of his photographs of St. Mark UMC in Mobile, AL.

My three children contributed, Glenda Ewbank Sealy, Shawn R. Ewbank and Todd C. Ewbank. Through my wife Betty DeVis Ewbank, I have also come to know and love her son, Rob Brandon. Without her encouragement this book would not have been finished and if so would not have been done as well.

Undoubtedly there are others who I have missed and I am sorry for the omission. You are appreciated.

Introduction

The first area of study in this book covers the organization of the United Methodist Church. It does not go into great detail but there is enough for the student to learn the basics of the Church. Some leaders may want to add more information in this or any other area as they work with their students.

The second area covers the history of our church. We have opted to start with Judaism, because our church has roots in the Old Testament and God's dealings with them. Next we look at the wonderful work of the church during its first 500 years and all the accomplishments we made during this early time. Then we move to the Protestant Reformation and briefly discuss some of the people and concepts of this time. Finally we discuss the Wesley's and later events leading to the uniting of the church to form the United Methodist Church.

The third area covers the beliefs of the United Methodist Church. This area uses the Articles of Religion which Wesley sent to America as a basis of the discussion. Of course we could have used a lot of other things but this is something all we Methodists should know.

The fourth and final area covers what we are to do as members of the United Methodist Church. There is no end to what can be used here to add to what is already covered.

I am not unaware of the question of sex as far as God goes, but for the sake of consistency I have always used the male description, but the female would work as well—didn't want to keep changing the sex of God.

All scriptures are from the New Revised Standard Version.

Tell Me About The United Methodist Church

Jim and Barb

Jim and Barb were deep in a dispute/discussion they had put off for a long time and were now having frequently. Recently transferred into a new community, they were looking to find some new friends for them and for their four year old—at least Barb was very interested, Jim seemed to have friends at work and he was pretty well satisfied with them.

When she discussed the situation with Jim her brown eyes were serious and her brunette hair managed to move uncontrollably around. Even with his flaming red hair Jim knew when Barb was really serious about something he did not stand a chance of changing her mind, and she would not allow any discussion about another topic until this one was exhausted and agreed upon

He was pretty happy with his work life during the week, as a manager at a local store, working around the house on Saturday, and then sleeping late and resting on Sunday. He did enjoy a game of golf now and then on Sunday with some of his friends. At 6' 4" and though right handed, he swung a golf club from the left side, he was a little tall for the best golf, but he had fun.

Barb did enjoy the big Sunday breakfasts they had at home or in a restaurant. However, she also thought they could and should decide on a church for their children and they should find their way back to church also. Besides their daughter, Glenda, was not baptized yet and they really should have that done.

Though attending different denominations when they were young their churches were part of an ecumenical youth group where they met. They went to the same high school. During their senior year they began dating and went steady later in the year.

They went to different colleges and pretty much lost contact with each other except for holidays and occasionally during the summer. In college both of them had been active in some of the extracurricular opportunities which were available, but not church. Somehow, with studying, classes, and their activities, church got left behind. After graduation they found one another again but lapsed in their attendance at church, thinking they were too busy launching careers and doing the things keeping young married couples busy.

Now however, at least to Barb, with one child and another on the way, and especially being new in a community, she had been seriously thinking and they had been talking about church for their children, and if for the children, also for themselves. Perhaps they could meet some new friends in the church which would be a bonus for them, particularly for Barb.

Glenda, their four year old, was a handful. Intelligent, questioning, and very determined and positive about what she wanted to do and when she wanted to do it. She had large brown eyes and brown hair which came half way down her back, pretty much a younger version of her mother. Barb was sure meeting and socializing with others her own age would be good for her. She would have to learn to share with a new one soon anyway, so why not start the process in church, she thought.

They had noticed a United Methodist Church just a few blocks away, so decided to take a look at it. One Saturday morning, Jim took a break from his yard work and thinking no one would probably be around the church at that time, they all got into the car and drove over to the church to see what they could see. They wanted to look the place over and see what it was like before making a final decision to go there and investigate further. The church was fairly easy to locate and they drove slowly by, turned around and as nobody seemed to be in the spacious parking lot, they drove in. The grounds were pretty well kept up and there were several buildings, so they decided to visit the church services the next day. After all, if they didn't like the services they could always try another church—there appeared to be several in the community, almost as many as there were drug stores and banks.

Being new and a little hesitant, they planned to and did arrive just before the services Sunday morning started and were able to slip into a pew towards the back of the church. After all, they did not know anybody and didn't want to get caught if they didn't like the atmosphere. Even though they arrived just before the start they had been greeted at the door of the church and the greeting had seemed to be real and well meant.

The services were all right and they liked Pastor Bill, as everybody seemed to call him. They slipped out a side door, but not before they were stopped by a few members of the congregation and were welcomed. All in all, they thought the entire trip had been a success. They saw in the bulletin the church had a Sunday School with classes for Glenda's age, so she could find some new friends there as she missed Abby the friend she left behind when they moved.

Reading the Church bulletin told them there were a lot of programs and events, so it seemed to be an active church. One activity going on was putting together health kits and flood buckets, whatever they were, for the United Methodist Committee on Relief (UMCOR). It seems they were put together to be shipped overseas to the needy there but also at times shipped in the United States as well. It also stated a committee was nearing completion of a study about a second and different type of church service and they would be making their recommendations to the church soon. It did not say exactly what type of service was planned, but the mere activity sounded interesting to them.

They were pleasantly surprised to receive a call on Wednesday saying the folks at St. Mark were happy to see them this past Sunday and hoped to see them next Sunday. Also if they had any specific needs a phone number was given. They decided right then to stop looking for other churches for comparison because they thought they would be happy at St. Mark.

They called the church to make an appointment to see Pastor Bill at a time which would be convenient for both of them. They were interested in finding out what they would have to do to join St. Mark.

An appointment was made for them and they arrived at the church to be greeted by the church secretary with cups of coffee. Pastor Bill was on his way from another meeting and he joined them very soon. They all settled down for a good chat.

Pastor Bill asked about Jim and Barb and their family, locations, children and ages and about their recent move, and desire to join the church. He was indeed easy to talk to and obviously was very interested in them.

He was a delightful mix. Well over six feet tall, probably in the neighborhood of 6' three or four, was balding with brown hair and wearing brown slacks with an open necked yellow shirt and a chain with a large wooden cross hanging down the front. He said he had received the cross as a gift at his ordination and he was very proud of it. His blue eyes sparkled as he talked about it.

He seemed to have a little of a southern drawl, even though he said he had graduated from Garrett-Evangelical Seminary, which is located on the campus of Northwestern University in Evanston, Illinois. He was born in a small Kansas town not far from Kansas City, called Baldwin, and was raised in Little Rock, Arkansas. Baldwin was also the location of Baker University, which is a Methodist college, and from which he graduated

Their discussion then turned to some of the many activities of the church. Jim and Barb talked about the churches they had attended when they were young and some of the activities they remembered. Barb said they had talked over and decided for the family to join one church rather than two in order to keep their family together.

Pastor Bill thought this decision represented very good thinking on their part. It certainly would be better for the family to stay together rather than go to separate churches and then try to figure out what to do with the children. The children would gain by being in one program rather than two and wondering why the other parent wasn't with them when they were together as a united family in everything else.

At this point Pastor Bill said it would be a good idea to take a break and look at the church's facilities. They first went through the Educational Building, which housed the church offices but also a lot of rooms for classes. In this building was an Early Learning Center (ELC), which took in the very young, almost from birth through four years of age. The Center taught these children what they could about the Christian life and living in general. There were children all over the area with their teachers and helpers. Pastor Bill said the ELC had terrific leadership and a great staff for the children. The other rooms were for Sunday School classes on Sunday but were used during the week by home school parents and children. These families worked together to provide the best education they could for their children.

They were surprised to see the church had a gym which was open at various times for youth in the community to come and play basketball. It was also used for other activities such as a place for huge garage sales and other community events.

The social center was nice and it had at one time been the sanctuary of the church until the present one was built. It was the location for a quilting group which met regularly for work and fun. Pastor Bill said they were soon going to have a second service there, an alternative service to try and bring in new members from the community who were not interested in the traditional service which they practiced in the sanctuary. A lot of thinking and plans had gone into the service and the church was now in the process of getting all of the necessary elements ready to begin. They were really looking forward to seeing how their efforts would turn out. They had great hopes for serving a broader community with this service.

The sanctuary featured a pretty stained glass window which had a picture of Jesus on it and contained several Christian symbols which Pastor Bill briefly explained. Beside the window with the picture of Jesus, which was behind the pulpit, there were stained glass windows on both sides of the sanctuary. The entry way or narthex had books which could be purchased and various other points of interest.

All of the buildings were clean and neat and gave the appearance that the congregation cared about how they looked.

This brought them back to the church offices. The entry had impressed them because there was a table, rug, lights, and pictures providing a comfortable setting. It really gave the entry a homey and welcoming appearance.

After continuing their discussion of the reasons for joining, they decided to take advantage of the membership class which Pastor Bill said would be starting in a few weeks. He told them he had two of these classes each year for new folks and members who wanted a refresher course. There were other classes on other topics as well which were regularly scheduled throughout the year and were well attended.

Jim and Barb were grateful Pastor Bill had shown so much interest in them and taken the time to show them about the location of the Sunday School classes for adults and for Glenda. He had told them to come a little early on Sunday mornings because the adults had coffee and other refreshments at the gathering place where they could meet and get to know some other members of the congregation. Those who attended Sunday School really looked forward to their time together before they broke into their regular classes.

On the way home Jim and Barb discussed their visit. They were pleased with what they knew about St. Mark UMC and looked forward to meeting some other young adults. They decided to just attend the worship services until they got started in the membership class. They might even find a friend or two in the class who was also in Sunday School and they could join them in their class. They also did not want to do too much too soon.

SCRIPTURE OF THE DAY

Make a joyful noise to the Lord, all the earth.
    Worship the Lord with gladness;
    come into his presence with singing.

Know that the Lord is God.
    It is he that made us and we are his;
    we are his people and the sheep of his pasture.

Enter his gates with thanksgiving,
    and his courts with praise,
    Give thanks to him, bless his name.

For the Lord is good;
    his steadfast love endures forever,
    and his faithfulness to all generations.
(Psalm 100)

PRAYER

Our Father, as we begin our study of what it means to be a Christian, guide our thoughts and open our hearts so we may think of you and your will for us and be receptive to what we learn about you.

We know you love us, each of us, and we are thankful. We know we have not earned your love but we rejoice in it.

Thank you for all you have done for us, the many blessings you have so freely given.

Bless those who begin this study and who finish it under your guidance so they may better understand and appreciate your mighty works on our behalf.

In the name of Christ we pray. Amen.

INTRODUCTION QUESTIONS

1. What problems were Jim and Barb wrestling with in deciding whether or not to seek a church?

2. What do you think was the deciding factor or factors of their choice to seek a church?

3. What about Pastor Bill's method of working with Jim and Barb, did you like it? Any methods or way he worked with them you did not like?

4. Did Jim and Barb look around as many people would in their search for a church? Discuss.

5. After their introduction to the Pastor and the church, would you look forward to the membership class? Why

CHAPTER 1 Organization of the United Methodist Church

A. Local Church—St. Mark United Methodist Church

Their first session of the membership class began pleasantly enough with coffee for some, cold sodas for others, and with several delicious cupcakes. They gathered in a circle of tables and Pastor Bill opened the class with a prayer for God's guidance for him and the understanding and sharing for them all and urging that they may all gain in their understanding about God, Jesus, the Holy Spirit, and the Christian life here at St. Mark.

In the coffee and introduction time Jim and Barb were pleasantly surprised to find Shawn and Diane and Todd and Melinda, other couples in the class, actually lived pretty close to them. Felista and James lived a little further away, but not too far so they all made plans for a get together soon for a dinner of grilled hamburgers and some hot dogs for the kids, or maybe just an ice cream supper.

Shawn and Diane were new to the community like themselves, arriving only four months before Jim and Barb. Todd and Melinda had been in the community some time and had just recently decided to try the church to see if it was something they really wanted to do. James and Felista Brown had been in another church but did not like it so they decided to try this church. The Brown's were an African American couple who seemed to be well known and thought of by those who knew them. She was in Real Estate and James Brown was a local attorney. There were several youth in the program as well, adding a lot of noise and activity to the classes. All in all it looked like an interesting group.

Pastor Bill began by discussing the church. St. Mark had a variety of organizations, programs, and opportunities for service and fellowship. He handed out materials which covered all of these programs, which included church services, Children's Church, Sunday School, and an area for preschool children where they were taken care of while their parents worshipped. Some of the other areas they discussed were choir, hand bells, ushers, greeters, the altar guild, and those who drove the busses and van to pick up the young and elderly. Other areas discussed were leading or helping in Sunday School classes, reading the Scripture in church services, and helping to prepare or serve communion.

Shawn said "I thought Sunday School was just for kids." When Shawn spoke his large, expressive brown eyes just danced and dimples appeared in his cheeks. He had a preference for khaki's when he did not have to dress up. Even his work clothes were khaki.

Diane, Shawn's wife spoke up "Don't pay any attention to Shawn he is just trying to find a reason to sleep late that's why he is talking about Sunday School being just for the kids."

"We've been going to Sunday School since coming to St. Mark and we enjoy the Fisher's Sunday School Class," Melinda said. "I like getting together before Sunday School and having coffee and refreshments and talking to the other adults who are in Sunday School."

Diane was the blonde of the group but she was definitely not an air head. In reality she had a very responsible job in a local business. With her blonde hair and dark blue eyes, she might remind one of a cheer leader in her time.

Two interesting organizations were also discussed. The United Methodist Women met regularly and had several circles, which composed their organization. The United Methodist Men met regularly for fellowship and service work. There were also activities for children and youth which the children could attend when some of them were a little older.

The church had other areas of service they could join because there were several additional committees of the church such as worship, pastoral relations, and finances, among others. The three emphases of the church were Leadership, Loving and Serving.

A Food Pantry group distributed food and at times gave financial help to the needy. The folks who ran this program were dedicated to helping others.

The church had a fairly unique ministry on Friday's. Coffee was prepared and donuts were purchased and they were given out free to those who stopped at the church by driving through the circular driveway. They called this ministry "Glazed Grace," a humorous, but serious way of describing what they did. A sign said they were given out free; however, if someone wished to talk the servers were happy to listen and pray with them. There was no hard sell, but if the visitor asked about the church the servers would happily tell them what they wanted to know, inform them of some of the church's activities, and invite them to come to the church services and any other activity they were interested in.

Our Methodist District opened a thrift store. Some of the original work to get the store open was done right here in our gym.

The store takes clothes, furniture, kitchen goods, jewelry, bedding, appliances, books and even automobiles. They are then put in the store for sale. The prices are low and the store is manned by volunteers. The best part about the store is that the earnings go to help local mission groups of the United Methodist Church.

"That's wonderful," said Barb, "I have some children's clothes I can give. Will they be able to use them?"

"Yes," replied Pastor Bill, "they will be happy to receive them."

Shawn said, "That's a wonderful way to use clothing that doesn't fit anymore. I have some clothing which is now too big for me and I would be willing to donate them to the cause."

"I have some dresses I don't wear anymore," said Melinda.

"You always have some dresses and other clothes you don't wear anymore," said Todd, and the others laughed.

Diane chimed in, "I have some clothes and jewelry I'd be happy to donate."

"Girl, don't you know I must have some clothes I'd like to donate to the store," said Felista. "I think it would be interesting to go to the store just to see what's there."

"Felista's never seen a store she didn't like," mumbled James.

"Where is this store," asked Barb, and Pastor Bill told them.

As far as how the membership services were organized and the subject of the sermons is concerned, he said pastors handle things quite differently. He wanted to present his ideas to the class so they could understand them, discuss them, and see how those ideas worked out in the church services and in the life of the church.

Though others have different views of worship and how many phases or movements were in worship, Pastor Bill said he believed the best description for him involved four phases.

The first phase or movement in worship is *adoration*. In this phase the primary object of our attention is God. This phase is one in which we adore God, who he is and what he has done for us. In worship we look at what we know about God and his perfectness. We are aware of God's love, his holiness, his justice, his mercy, his righteousness, his steadfastness, and all the qualities we see and know in God.

We come to worship services usually involved in our own cares and jobs and concerns, so the first thing we have to do is to look outside ourselves.

Any aspect of God, any adoration we want to make of or to God is acceptable during this phase of worship. We are brought out of our lives, our concerns, our hopes, and our fears to contemplate God. He is the Creator of all that is including us and he is also our redeemer. God is still working in the world. We can think of God and his healing power and his involvement in all our lives.

We think of God's love, a love so unique that it is hard to even find words to express it. He called the Jews from out of the many peoples of the earth to be a beacon for the rest of humanity and a blessing for them. He entered into a covenant or agreement with them saying he would be their God if they would be His people.

He agreed to be their God and even though they did not always keep their part, his love for them continued. God was steadfast in his love and covenant. Now we have become a people of God through Jesus Christ. Think of the love it took to send his only Son to earth to live among us and teach us and then to die for us so God could claim the victory over sin and death for us through the work of his Son. Think of the incredible love it took to do this for us!

We can also think of God's steadfastness. God has made covenants with His people and he has kept his part of the agreement even when we did not. He was steadfast in his care and concern for the Jews even when they rebelled. He never gave up on them as his people.

He has loved and had so much mercy that even though humanity and all creation has fallen and become estranged from him, He found a way to overcome our sinful separation from him by sending his only Son to earth, to be born a child, to live among us and teach us, and eventually to die on a cross for us so we could, by God's grace, be reconciled to him.

What love, what justice, what mercy, what righteousness, what steadfastness—that God would do all this for us—for you and for me!

There is so much we can adore about God and his great works on our behalf we could spend hours just on this phase alone. However, in our service of worship this is only the first phase.

The next phase is *confession*, and in it we turn our attention from adoring God to looking at ourselves. By comparison we find we are sinful, hurtful, and a stiff-necked people. We do not love as we ought, we are not merciful as we should be, we do not worship God as he should be worshipped, and we do not love our needy fellow humans as we should.

In fact it is not just we alone, it is our entire society, our social institutions, and even our churches are full of sinful people who are separated from God and his kingdom. Christians are sinners who want and seek the forgiveness of God and his help to become better Christians.

This phase compares God's qualities with ours, what God wants for us and created us to be, and we find ourselves lacking. We feel compelled to confess our sins, shortcomings, and trespasses because we have seen God revealed to us through his Son. We confess because though we were created to be in the image of God, we fall far short of the image and only by God's grace is the image in process of being restored in us.

In fact the confession we use in the introduction of the Lord's Supper says it all:
Merciful God,
We confess that we have not loved you with our whole heart.
We have failed to be an obedient church.
We have not done your will,
we have broken your law,
we have rebelled against your love, we have not loved our neighbors,
 and we have not heard the cry of the needy.
Forgive us, we pray.
Free us for joyful obedience,
Through Jesus Christ our Lord. Amen.[1]

The third phase of our worship service is *illumination* and it covers the sermon, Scripture and areas in which God is speaking to us about our lives—what we are to change, what we should do, and how we can come closer to God. Our pathway or life as Christians is being illuminated and being made clear. The Word of God, Christ, speaks to us through the Scriptures and sermon telling us how we were created to be, to live and how to become closer to God and be a better servant of his. This phase of worship helps us understand more about God and about being a Christian.

---

[1] *The United Methodist Hymnal*, 12

"At least it's what I am supposed to be doing and I really try hard to do it," said Pastor Bill. "Of course the sermon can be on any topic which relates Scripture to life or life to Scripture so there is a wide well to draw inspiration from."

After receiving the Word of God for our lives we come to the fourth and last phase of worship which is *dedication*. We have seen God and the wonderfulness of our Creator, we have seen we are not who God wanted and wants for us, we have seen God wants much more for us than we are now and have now, so now we dedicate or rededicate our lives to becoming better Christians. This is one reason why our offering is after the sermon because the sermon is in the illumination phase and the offering is in the dedication phase of worship.

Todd joined in "I had no idea so much thought went into the outline of the service. I thought the service was copied out of a book or something."

"I was surprised there were phases in the worship services. Even though I hadn't thought about it at all, after hearing it explained, it makes sense to me now," said Melinda.

Todd said "Now I will be much more aware of the phases of worship. I am really happy to know more about it and it will help me when we are in Church."

"This is the very reason I took so much time in explaining it," Pastor Bill said, "because this is the way I understand worship, our services on Sunday are organized to follow these four phases of worship."

Jim responded "I will never look at the service of worship the same again because I did not realize the service was organized in any particular manner."

Todd and Shawn agreed with Jim's comment and Diane, Barb, Felista and James expressed their thanks for the new appreciation of the flow of the church service.

They took a short break to think over what they had been told before moving on to the next area of thought.

When everybody had returned to their seats Pastor Bill said St. Mark followed the Christian Year, but we were willing to and did change a particular Sunday if there was an emergency, or event requiring it. By planning the year's services he was able to make sure he didn't get into a rut or habit of preaching on the same or similar themes and all areas of the Christian life received attention. He said while he was on vacation each year he planned the themes and

Scriptures for the year. Naturally he did not write the sermons completely out then but he did add to each theme topic books to read, Scriptures which might be appropriate, and during the year he could add thoughts or something he read to any of the upcoming Sunday's sermons. He kept a folder for each Sunday and just put the notes and other items in the appropriate folder.

Pastor Bill said he was not giving a test or anything on the calendar year of the church, often called the Liturgical Year, but can you think of any time during a year which would definitely be on the church calendar?

After a pause Barb said, "Do you mean something like Christmas and Easter or were you thinking of other things like the Fourth of July?"

Jim said, "I guess we're not talking about April Fool's Day or Halloween, are we?"

"You are exactly right," said Pastor Bill. "Now we are going to go a little deeper into the church year so you can understand it. We have copies of the explanation of the church year and they are in your packet for today. You are welcome to take it home and keep it if you want to. There is a copy hanging in the church narthex or entry of the church, and also in the Sunday School area on their bulletin board. Each of these copies has a marker on them which shows where we are in the church year."

There are two cycles to the church year which are built around the two great Christian events which Barb mentioned. The Christmas cycle is composed of Advent, Christmas, and Epiphany and the Easter cycle is composed of Lent, Easter, and Pentecost. In looking at them you can see immediately there is a season immediately before Christmas and Easter which is a yearning for or preparation time before the main event of each portion of the church year. There is also a season after the main event.

The first cycle built around Christmas covers such themes as the incarnation of Jesus and his ministry. The second cycle built around Easter covers the birth of the church and the coming of the kingdom of God.

"Now let's take a look at the first cycle built around Christmas," said Pastor Bill.

Advent, as we all know is primarily a season of expectancy. The expectancy is for the coming of the promised one, our savior. We are looking forward to his arrival and all this event would mean for us. It covers four Sunday's, and ends with Christmas Eve.

Naturally we then have Christmas and all of the preparations for it. Christmas is the birth of Jesus, the long expected and waited for Savior. He is here and God did something we would never have thought of or considered. The Savior came to us as a child, God's Son born by a human female, Mary. This child was fully human and fully divine and we will talk more about this later in our classes. This season covers the nativity of Jesus.

Epiphany begins with the first Sunday of the year and continues until Lent, which is the start of the next cycle. Epiphany is the season of the evangel and it continues until Ash Wednesday. Because of the moving dates of Easter, the exact number of Sunday's in Epiphany changes. The themes we can expect to be explored are Christ as the light of the world which should give to us, his disciples, a world-wide vision, a social and missionary emphasis.

"Now let's go on to the second cycle which is built around Easter," said Pastor Bill.

We begin with Lent which is the season of renewal and goes from Ash Wednesday to Easter. The main themes which are covered in this season are the renewal of our lives through repentance and redemption.

In this period are special times such as Holy Week—the passion and triumph of Jesus, Maundy Thursday—and Good Friday—the meaning of the cross. The themes expected to be explored during this time are the Holy Spirit, the doctrine of God, our response of commitment to God, the church and Kingdom loyalties of Christians. For Easter naturally we will explore the meaning and significance of the resurrection.

During Pentecost we explore the themes of life as a church, the patriarchs, Kings and prophets.

"It's break time again because we have covered a lot and are in need of time to discuss and download the information we have received," said Pastor Bill.

All were grateful for the break because they had received a lot of information and it was interesting for them to discuss these ideas they had learned with the other class members.

"I really did not think about a church year or that the church even had a year," said Todd. "I knew about Easter and Christmas but did not realize the rest of the year had meaning also."

Diane said, "I didn't either. I did not realize the whole year was tied together in this manner."

"The church year makes a lot of sense to me," said Melinda, "and I'm happy to know more about it. By knowing about the church year you know more about what is happening and what is going to happen."

Todd and Melinda are an interesting couple. He is just over 6' tall but very thin and wore his hair long. He has a great smile and uses it often. His blue eyes set off his brown hair. His looks made you think he could be a model.

Melinda on the other hand, was a blonde only because of her hair dresser's work but it looked very nice and did set off her green eyes. One hardly recognized she seemed to think before she made a comment and sometimes had a small stutter to get started. Both of them were locally employed.

"I thought there were more times in the church year because I remember something about Whitsuntide or something like that," said Shawn.

"There were more times during the church year in the past, but it has been streamlined somewhat now," Pastor Bill Said, "and the times we've just discussed are the most popular."

Felista said "I was glad there were no more terms than those we have just covered."

Her husband James nodded and said, "I agree with that assessment."

"Spoken just like a lawyer James," said Felista.

When they had reconvened Pastor Bill said they would spend a little time on church colors. Each Sunday in the church year has a color. Pastor Bill said these colors would be on the stole he wore each Sunday. The choir also changed the colors of their stoles.

He said he would now hand out a piece of paper with the church colors listed on one side and the definitions given on the other. They are mixed up however, so read them and see if you can guess or infer which color goes with each definition. When all have finished we will discuss them and see how well we have done. The class industriously went to work with a lot of sighing and laughing as they marked their papers. The colors and definitions they were given are shown on the next page.

Purple	Is the color of hope
White	Is the color of growth
Red	Is the color for both penance and royalty
Green	Is the color of fire, symbolizing the Holy Spirit, also the color of blood
Blue	Is the color of joy and festivity
Gold	Is the color of death and resurrection

After he had given the group several minutes to work Barb raised her hand and said she thought she was able to get them all correct. She told the group that her reasoning went this way. Purple is obviously the color of royalty so this takes care of the first color. Red has to be for fire and blood and Green must be for growth. This takes care of the first three and the second three are more difficult but she thought she was correct on them also. If you make White for death and resurrection, and you make Gold for festivity and joy, then Blue has to be the color of hope. Pastor Bill said she had done great work and she was 100% right. Everyone in the class clapped for her great efforts.

This is how it looks when completed as Barb said.

Purple	Penance and Royalty
White	Death and Resurrection
Red	Fire and Blood
Green	Growth
Blue	Hope
Gold	Joy and Festivity

Diane said, "I wish I'd thought of it that way. I tried to get them all together instead of looking at them in individually as Barb did. It does make a lot of sense when you look at it like she did."

"I wondered why the choir changed their stoles," mused Todd, "I thought they must be dirty and needed cleaning."

Barb said "I've seen the choir and pastor change colors but did not know what it meant. I'm glad to know more about it now."

"Not only a church year but colors as well. I'll bet the colors are tied in with the church year, aren't they Pastor Bill," said Todd.

"You are right and the copies of the church year which keep track of where we are also has the colors for each Sunday," said Pastor Bill. "However some ministers follow these colors and some do not. In our case we do."

B. District

After a short break, Pastor Bill said St. Mark is known as St. Mark United Methodist Church and those last three words of its name made a world of difference between St. Mark and many other churches. They were going to join St. Mark UMC and St. Mark was not a standalone church. Almost everybody knows they are joining the local church and become a member of the congregation, but some members may not realize by joining the local church they have become a part of a much larger group. They have become part of a district, an annual conference, a jurisdiction, the General Church, and churches and annual conferences around the world.

Groups of Methodist churches in an area are organized to form a district. Each district is led by a district superintendent or a D.S., who is an elder of the church and appointed by the Bishop in the area. Their term is usually for six years but it may be shortened or somewhat lengthened for reason. The D.S. acts as a kind of pastor to the pastors in their district as well as performs many other leadership duties.

The district also has a number of committees, some of which are echoed by the same or similar committee in the local church. Examples of this are local and district Lay Leaders, local and district United Methodist Women, and local and district United Methodist Men. The district has some committees the local church does not have such as a committee on nominations (though the local church has a committee which performs similar functions), a committee on the ministry which works with individuals who think they have received a call to ministry and to those who are in school preparing for the ministry. There is also a committee on the superintendency, though again it is somewhat like the pastoral relations committee at the local church.

Jim asked, "Where is our D.S. located?"

Pastor Bill replied, "We're lucky because the D.S. in our district is housed in our city and has an office in town for business."

"That is good information to know," said Melinda.

The D.S. works through the year to be pastor to the pastors in the district by meeting with them in various settings, counsels with them on a variety of topics, as well as relays to them information which has been given to them by the church, the Bishop or conference. The D.S. may meet with people from the churches in the district, discussing a variety of concerns.

Once a year the D.S. meets with the local church and pastor in what is called a charge conference. A charge is the church or churches served by a minister. The charge conference reports on the health of the charge with such information as projects and programs initiated or completed, people to be added or removed from the rolls of the church, and the appointment of officers and leaders in the church for the next year. This meeting is a large undertaking and very important for the local church.

The D.S. often has training sessions of one type or another; many of them are to educate the pastors on new ideas. Also new initiatives for the district or local churches are led by the D.S. in support of new programs.

Methodist ministers unlike ministers from other denominations are moved from one church to another and are appointed to serve a charge one year at a time. In order to accomplish this massive undertaking our local D.S. meets with the other D.S.'s in the conference and the resident Bishop. The Bishop and the D.S.'s with some others are called the cabinet. The cabinet determines annually where every United Methodist pastor shall serve for the next year— whether to stay or to move to another location in the conference.

This is called the itinerant system and has been the accepted method of getting ordained elders, provisional elders, and associate members disbursed to the available areas of service. It would be highly likely that if we had a "call" system like some other denominations, in which each church issues a "call" to a minister, some of our churches would be without pastors and some of our pastors would not have churches. Our way uses the prayerful talents of the Bishop and D.S.'s, in conjunction with the desires and uniqueness's of individual churches, and the desires and talents of the pastors to try our human best under the direction of the Holy Spirit to get the best possible matches throughout the conference. Naturally among other considerations the salaries of the pastor and prospective church are considered.

"Guess you don't get to totally unpack due to the possibility of moving," Todd laughed.

Diane spoke thoughtfully "I know of some pastors who spent a long time in one place."

Pastor Bill replied "True, not every minister moves every year. In fact some have been in the same charge for many years. However, they are still appointed to the charge every year."

Pastor Bill said the United Methodist Church is guided by a book called "The Book of Discipline of the United Methodist Church." Obviously we do not really call it by such a long name. We usually refer to it as the Book of Discipline or just Discipline for short. The Discipline outlines the rules and organization which must be followed by all local churches but within those rules and guidelines there often is room for the local church to express its unique ministry in order for it to fit the community and the local church. The Discipline was first written many years ago and in fact he showed them a collection of them he had, one of which was published in 1856. This particular Discipline was called "The Doctrines and Discipline of the Methodist Episcopal Church," and belonged to his grandfather who was also a Methodist Minister. It is much smaller and contained many different topics back then. As we have matured as a church we have required our Discipline to reflect these differences and as a result our current ones are more than double the size of this earlier one.

"Discipline, sounds like something bad," said Shawn, "it sounds like we have done something wrong and are going to be chastised for doing it."

Diane with her blue eyes flashing said "you have to understand discipline as doing things the right way so you discipline yourself, not because you were bad but to be correct."

"Oh right," said Shawn, "the other definition of discipline which we don't normally think about or use."

"For example", Pastor Bill said, "the Book of discipline tells us what mandatory committees we must have and those we could have as well as offices we must fill and some we can fill. Other committees and organizations are either suggested or left up to the local church to decide what they want. The reason for such diversity in unity is the needs of various churches. Some are very large, many are small, some are in one area and others are in an entirely different area and serve an entirely different group of people."

There are only four committees which are mandatory for each church to have. They are the Pastoral Relations Committee, the Finance Committee, the Nominations and Leadership Development Committee, and the Board of Trustees.

The Pastoral Relations Committee or Staff Parish Relations Committee keeps the pastor informed about the church and the church's concerns and informs the church about the pastor and the pastor's concerns. It also handles troubles which concern the pastor or paid workers of the church as well as recommends the return or not return of the pastor for another year. This committee is also responsible for evaluating prospective employees and recommending hiring. The salaries of the pastor and church employees are also a part of this committee's work.

The Finance Committee is responsible to oversee the financial health of the church. They are responsible for creating a budget for the church and make other needed financial recommendations.

Pastor Bill said, "In our church, our budget is 80% of what we think we will receive and if we receive the 100% of what we think we will, we have a wonderful reserve to use the next year for many projects. This way we don't get behind in our budget and we can plan wonderful activities for our church for the next year."

The Nominations and Leadership Development Committee focuses on missions and ministry throughout the year. They are best known for their work of seeking out and nominating officers for the next year. This is a very important work to try to match the skills and interests of the members with the positions of leadership they need to fill.

The Board of Trustees is the fourth group each church must have. They handle the real and personal property of the church. They work to keep the property of the church in good, responsible order. Because our church has several buildings and they are used for many activities, this is a constant job for them.

The Church Council is composed of these four groups, and any others the local church may decide to have. They work together to create effective programs of nurture, outreach and witness for the church. It continually evaluates and seeks to improve the work of the church. All groups or committees share their plans and results with the Council.

SCRIPTURE OF THE DAY

The gifts he gave were that some would be apostles, some prophets, some evangelists, some pastors and teachers, to equip the saints for the work of ministry, for building up the body of Christ, until all of us come to the unity of the faith and of the knowledge of the Son of God, to maturity, to the measure of the full stature of Christ. We must no longer be children, tossed to and fro and blown about by every wind of doctrine, by people's trickery, by their craftiness in deceitful scheming. But speaking the truth in love, we must grow up in every way into him who is the head, into Christ, from whom the whole body, joined and knit together by every ligament with which it is equipped, as each part is working properly, promotes the body's growth in building itself up in love. (Ephesians 4:11-16)

PRAYER

Our heavenly Father, we give you thanks for your love which sent the Son into the world not to condemn the world but that the world might be saved through him. We thank you for the church which exists even today in his name and for his sake.

We participate in His Church today and are trying to learn more about You, your Son, and Holy Spirit, and our proper response to that knowledge and awareness.

Be with us this day as we learn and share our thoughts and ideas with one another so it all may be done under your guidance and for our sake.

We ask these things in the name of Christ. Amen.

CHAPTER 1. QUESTIONS

1. What are some of the organizations of the church and what do they do?

2. Discuss the four phases of worship. Do you agree with these phases or do you have other ideas?

3. Describe and discuss the Christian Year. Does the Christian Year make more sense to you now you are more aware of it?

4. What do you think about the colors used in churches and their significance?

5. How do the local church and the district relate to one another?

6. What are some of the duties of the District Superintendent?

7. What is the Book of Discipline of the United Methodist Church?

CHAPTER 2 Organization of the Methodist Church (cont.)

C. Annual Conference

As they gathered in the class room, the group was still talking about the organization of the local church and how all the parts fit together.

Todd said "I'm really impressed by the fact ministers are subject to being moved every year, I wonder how they all handle it."

Melinda's green eyes flashed when she responded "They may be subject to being moved but it doesn't mean they will be."

"You tell him girl," said Felista. "They can't move all of them in one year. That would just be too much of a fruit basket upset. Besides how are the churches going to pay for such a mass move?"

"I'm interested in the organization of the church beyond the local church" Shawn stated. "That looks like an interesting area to me."

Diane said "I'm interested in that too. I also want to know how many people and organizations are involved. Most large denominations have some organization at the top which make decisions for them. It would be interesting to see how all that works out here in the Methodist Church."

Pastor Bill, who had just entered the room and heard some of the discussion, said they would now see if they could get some answers to their questions.

The Bishop is not located or housed in our district though the Bishop supervises and is a pastor to the D.S.'s in the area as well as performing the same duties for all of the pastors in the district he or she oversees. The area a Bishop oversees is called an Episcopal Area.

A group of districts form a conference and the Bishop is the supervisory or Episcopal head of the conference. An annual conference involves all the churches in the districts in the Bishop's area. Some Bishops oversee more than one conference, which means they have double duties of a sort, or the same responsibilities in each of their areas.

When we use the term "annual conference" it can be a little slippery because it can mean more than one thing. First use of the term annual conference is to mean what the Book of Discipline describes as the "basic unit" of the Methodist Church. It is the area covered by the particular annual conference. As we discussed earlier, geographically an annual conference can be a state, or part of a state or as in our case, a part of two states.

Secondly, sometimes when we refer to the annual conference we are really referring to the organization or the professional staff which have been brought together to conduct ministry and the affairs of the conference. Probably most of them have such staff as are needed to direct the connectional ministries, a treasurer, directors of various program areas, and other staff which are deemed appropriate or required by the Book of Discipline. Both clergy and lay persons may serve on some of these groups. These staff members work year round for the conference and are indispensable to the effective work of the conference.

The third use of the term annual conference refers to the annual meetings. Members from each church as well as the pastors attend these sessions which run from 3-5 days. They gather for worship, fellowship, and also to conduct the business of the conference. Though anyone may attend these sessions the voting delegates which have been selected from each church and the pastors, in equal number are the only ones who can vote. Reports of past and ongoing work within the conference, future goals, programs, and budgets are presented. We also elect delegates to the Jurisdictional and General Conferences. Fortunately we only have to elect delegates every four years because these elections take a lot of additional time.

Our own annual conference used to be longer but we have found ways to reduce it. We now start on Sunday evening and complete our work around noon on Wednesday.

Part of the work of the annual conference concerns the ministers. It covers such areas as how ministers get into the conference, stay in the conference, transfer to other conferences or from other conferences to ours, how they are paid, their retirement plans, health benefits, when they retire etc.

"In fact," Pastor Bill said, "as ministers in the United Methodist Church we are members of our annual conference, not members of local churches."

The annual conference also handles the churches such as which district they are in, whether they are a standalone church or are joining with another church or churches, and the appointment of pastors for the next year are formalized.

If there are any constitutional amendments they are voted on by the annual conference.

The committees report on other work and discuss future plans. Fortunately this is usually printed in a large booklet called the Brochure of Reports which is distributed before the conference and can be read by the delegates beforehand; however, often presentations are made anyway. Then the Conference Journal is printed later which has all of the information in the Brochure of Reports which has been agreed to by the conference as well as the other actions taken by the conference.

Finally, the Annual Conference sets priorities for the ministers and the budgets for the conference.

Barb said, "I've been given a lot of information to digest and I'm not entirely clear by what it means to be appointed."

Pastor Bill said, "That is a good question. Let's see if we can answer it."

United Methodist ministers are appointed each year for a one year term to work at a particular location. Where they are appointed is called a charge and that is why a charge conference was mentioned before. You see our system started many years ago. In our Discipline the itinerancy system is the way in which all ministers are appointed and it is stated all ministers must agree to abide by this system.[2] It is a procedure whereby the Bishop and the cabinet try to get the best talents of the ministers to the needs of each church.

Jim then asked, "Is it possible you will have to move next year, Pastor Bill?"

He responded by saying, "I've been at St. Mark for only two years and it is very unlikely I will be moved because the normal stay for pastors is longer. However," he said "I cannot promise you I will not be moved. Our appointments, as you know, are made for only one year but I would be very surprised if a change was made."

Melinda said and Todd agreed. "We are glad you probably won't be moved," and the others, nodded their heads.

Shawn said, "I have never been to an annual conference but after hearing so much about them I would like to attend at least once just to see what it is like."

"Me too," agreed Diane.

"The annual conference is the basic working body of the church but there are other conferences with their own duties and responsibilities," said Pastor Bill.

---

[2] *Discipline*, 264

"There are more," questioned Diane, "What a lot of conferences." "Oh, that's right," she further stated, "They only meet every four years. That's not too often, is it?"

Shawn said "It's often enough for me," but Melinda wondered, "Is it often enough for them to do the work of the church, even congress meets every year?"

D. Other Conferences, Committees and Counsels

Pastor Bill began by saying the Jurisdictional Conference does not cover the entire church. It represents only a part of the church. The United States is made up of five jurisdictions. We happen to be in the Southeastern Jurisdiction. It meets every four years and deals with matters within the jurisdiction, as well as moving Bishops from one jurisdiction to another. This conference has agencies and committees to do a lot of the work for them much like the annual conference.

The Jurisdictional Conference is where Bishops come from. They are elected by this conference and they are assigned to Episcopal Areas by the Conference. It also determines the boundaries of annual conferences and Episcopal areas.

The General Conference has from 600 to 1,000 members who are equally divided between the ministry and the laity. It defines the powers and duties of all levels of ministry and works on the hymnal and our ritual. It also makes sure there are Boards and Committees to perform the work of the Church

General Conference meets every four years during April or May and this conference is the legislative body of the church. The last meetings were in 2016, 2012, and 2008. As he said before, the members to this conference are elected by the annual conferences. This is the only group which can speak for the United Methodist Church. No Bishop or group of Bishops, and no agency or committee of the church has the power to speak for the church. Only the General Conference can speak for the entire church.

The work of the General Conference is hectic. It accepts petitions from any organization, pastor, or lay member of the United Methodist Church. This amounts to two weeks of very full days of studying the petitions and trying to decide if they are acceptable and in any case, how they may change other portions of the Book of Discipline. If a petition is processed it will result in changes to the Book of discipline. This is what Pastor Bill meant when he commented the Book of Discipline is rewritten every four years. There are delegates and alternate delegates to this conference to assure no part of the church will be without representation in these discussions.

The Social Principles of the United Methodist Church are a prayerful and thoughtful effort of the General Conference to consider how the gospel interacts with different cultural contexts. They are printed in "The Book of Resolutions."

The Social Principles are divided into areas of consideration. They are:

The Natural World – uses and abuses of it.

The Nurturing Community – new forms of community, nurture, and evaluation.

The Social Community – all people are created by God, there should be no discrimination.

The Economic Community – these systems are under God's judgment.

The Political Community – Governments are responsible for their people. Neither Church nor State is to be dominant.

The World Community – God's world is one, there should be no divisions.

Both of these conferences are in the same year with the General Conference early in the year and the Jurisdictional Conference later in the year.

There is a Judicial Council in our church which is elected by the General Conference and it makes sure any actions voted on by the General Conference are constitutional. It acts as the judiciary arm of the church.

There is also a Council of Bishops which includes all Bishops, active or retired, who provide leadership and vision for the whole church.

The United Methodist Church has a lot of commissions and boards which perform a massive amount of work for the church. Pastor Bill said he would hand out a sheet with the names of the commissions etc. on one side and the definitions on the other. He wanted to see how well they could guess the work of each group. He said most of them are pretty well explanatory.

This is what was on the paper Pastor Bill handed out.
General Commission on Religion and Race
General Commission on Status and Role of Women
General Commission on Communication
United Methodist Publishing House

General Council on Finance and Administration
General Board of Global Ministries
General Board of Discipleship
General Board of Church and Society
General Commission on Archives and History
General Commission on Christian Unity and Interreligious Concerns
General Board of Higher Education and Ministry
General Board of Pensions and Health Benefits
General Commission on United Methodist Men

    1. Gathers, preserves, and disseminates materials on the history of the United Methodist Church and its antecedents. It maintains archives and a library in which the historical records are kept.

    2. Provides leadership for the denomination in the fields of communication, public relations, and promotion of the general funds and programs of the denomination. It is the official news gathering and distribution agency of the denomination. It provides resources and services to local churches and annual conferences in the field of communications.

    3. Advocates for and works toward Christian unity in every aspect of the life of the United Methodist Church. It works to enable ecumenical and interreligious understanding and experience among all United Methodists.

    4. Distributes all the official publications, records and forms of the denomination, publishes books through Abingdon Press, and operates Cokesbury retail and online stores, and mail order service. It also publishes and distributes church school materials and resources throughout the denomination.

    5. Focused on bringing about full and equal participation of the racial and ethnic constituencies in The United Methodist Church. The commission carries out its work through advocacy of the issues and by reviewing and monitoring the practices of the denomination.

    6. Administers the finances and operational needs of the denomination and serves as the general treasurer of the denomination.

    7. Prepares and assists people to fulfill their ordained ministries and to provide general oversight for campus ministries and institutions of higher learning.

    8. Provides leadership and resources in the areas of spiritual growth and development, devotional literature, curriculum resources,

Christian education, evangelism, worship, stewardship, and ministry of the laity. It also oversees The Upper Room.

9. Involves men in a growing relationship to Jesus Christ and his church and to provide resources and support for programs of evangelism, stewardship and the needs of men.

10. Responsible to witness to Jesus Christ throughout the world, to recruit and send missionaries, to raise the awareness and support of persons in local churches for global mission, and to assist in the development of Christian churches and leadership.

11. Supervises and administers the pension and benefits programs, plans, and funds of The United Methodist Church. It administers and disburses the retirement and benefit funds of the various annual conferences.

12. Challenges United Methodists to work in areas of important social concern and develops resources to inform, motivate, and train United Methodists on issues of social justice in the society.

13. Challenges the United Methodist Church to a commitment to the full participating of women in the complete life and mission of the church. The commission serves as an advocate for and on behalf of women, seeks to eliminate inequalities in relation to women in the church, and monitors the general agencies, institutions, and connectional structures to ensure inclusiveness of women.

Shawn, Todd, Diane, Melinda, Jim, Barb, Felista and James gathered at one table to work out the answers. 'Oh my goodness" said Barb, "that's quite a group. How in the world will we be able to get all this put together?"

"Well, let's get started and see how far we can go," said Diane, and they began.

They quickly decided to divide up the work and each person would only have to get two right and they would have more than enough. Each one took three of the commissions and looked for the proper definitions giving them two people working on many questions.

It didn't take long and they were able to raise their hands with what they thought were the correct answers.

Their answers were as follows:
The General Commission on Religion and Race is number 5;
The General Commission on the Status and Role of Women is number 13;
The General Commission on Communication is number 2;
The United Methodist Publishing House is number 4;

The General Counsel on Finance and Administration is number 6;
The General Board of Global Ministries is number 10;
The General Board of Discipleship is number 8;
The General Board of Church and Society is number 12;
The General Commission on Archives and History is number 1;
The General Board on Christian Unity and Interreligious Concerns is number 3;
The General Board of Higher Education and Ministry is number 7;
The General Board of Pensions and Health Benefits is number 11;
The General Commission on United Methodist Men is number 9.

Since their group was first and were told they had all of them correct, they were given a hand by the others in the class. They thought the way they had organized their research and then compared notes to make sure they had no duplications was a good way to solve the questions. They also all agreed it was a lengthy job, was not terribly hard and they learned a lot by going through it and sharing their findings with the rest of the group.

"One could spend a lot of time studying the organization of our church and our study this far is not complete, but we will have to move on if we ever want to finish," said Pastor Bill. "By the way, a lot of this information is on the website of the United Methodist Church, which you can look up later and study to your heart's content. The website is http://www.umc.org and it provides an abundance of information."

He said he'd made all of the organizations, positions, and duties as simple and understandable as possible and still be faithful to them.

One further thing about the church is all church property is held in trust. All property of local churches and other agencies and institutions is held for the benefit of the entire denomination, not by the local church. All property must be used in accordance with the Discipline. This has been our agreement since 1797 when it was made a part of that Discipline.

This way of controlling property reflects the connectional structure of the Church and assures our property will be used only for purposes consistent with the mission of the entire denomination. The mission of the Church is to make disciples of Jesus Christ for the transformation of the world, and we believe this disciple making primarily takes place at the local church level.

The Discipline says this method of handling property allows for the "fundamental expression of United Methodism whereby local churches and other agencies and institutions within the denomination are both held accountable to and benefit from their connection with the entire worldwide Church."

In fact the titles to property are not held by The United Methodist Church, the General Conference, or Jurisdictional Conference. These titles are held at a lower level of the denomination. Most of them are held by incorporated conferences, agencies, or organizations.

It is a way of tying all of our local churches and church organizations together. About everything outside the local church is paid for by the local church. They are called assessments which the local annual conference decides how to distribute to the local churches.

Jim said, "I did not realize how many organizations or Church Boards and Committees the United Methodist Church had."

"The Church is certainly more organized than I thought," said Diane.

Felista said, "I had no idea the church was so well organized. Wish I had that kind of organization working for me."

"Amen," said James, and the others laughed..

Todd wondered aloud "are all of these organizations needed or is there a lot of duplication of some type?"

"I guess they are all needed," said Melinda "or they probably wouldn't have them. I don't see how you could drop any of these and still cover the area they do now."

"Of course" Barb said," we don't know how many people are in each of these organizations but I went on the internet at the United Methodist Church website and found several publications and different areas, even within some of these organizations."

"Wow" said Shawn, "that would give them a lot of coverage, more than I knew before."

Felista said, "This sounds like the organizations Jim continually wants to join, and I have no earthly idea why he would want to do it."

"Just like these organizations, Felista, they are all important and necessary," said Jim.

"I'm about ready for a new topic," said Todd. "The organization is interesting but I'd like to get into some other areas also."

SCRIPTURE

Now you are the body of Christ and individually members of it. And God has appointed in the church first apostles, second prophets, third teachers; then deeds of power, then gifts of healing, forms of assistance, forms of leadership, various kinds of tongues. Are all apostles? Are all prophets? Are all teachers? Do all work miracles? Do all possess gifts of healing? Do all speak in tongues? Do all interpret? But strive for the greater gifts. And I will show you a still more excellent way.
(I Corinthians 12:27-31)

PRAYER

Our Father, your gifts are gracious and many. You have distributed your gifts throughout our congregation and group so we are not all alike, but rather we complement each other and fulfill each other. We give you praise for your work of preparing us for Christian living.

Be with us as we study together to learn about your church, its organization, and the part all of us may play in preparing the way for your kingdom.

We are thankful to have the opportunity to gather together without fear as do some who meet in your name.

Bless us we pray. Amen.

CHAPTER 2. QUESTIONS

1. What is the Annual Conference? It can be considered one of three things. What are they?

2. Who gets to attend the Annual Conference? Can all attendees vote?

3. What kinds of business does the Annual Conference transact?

4. What is the difference between the General Conference and the Jurisdictional Conference?

5. Name two of the General Boards or Commissions and their function?

CHAPTER 3 History of the United Methodist Church (cont.)

A. Jewish Background

As the group began gathering Barb and Diane started talking about the party they had for some of the members of the class. Homemade ice cream went down very well in the hot evening. There was vanilla and strawberry and both adults and kids ate their fill. Felista and Jim brought some cookies they had made, and Melinda brought a pound cake. They had enjoyed it and even the younger ones who came were very polite and seemed to have a good time.

Felista told them, "We bought a new washing machine and dryer and when I was running the first load it started jumping around so I hopped on it and it still jumped around carrying me with it around the laundry room. I finally got Jim away from his books and he turned the machine off and found some thing a ma bobs in the bottom had not been released as they should have. Jim said it was something about anchor bolts not taken off or something like that."

They all laughed at the picture of Felista being taken around the laundry room by a machine.

When Melinda and Todd came in she said "the next area on the history of the United Methodist Church looks very interesting to us."

Todd said, "I was a little surprised they began the history of the church with the Old Testament. I thought we would probably start with the Methodist Church in America."

"I got a kick out of reading in the Old Testament," said Felista. "I haven't read it all but some of the stories I certainly had heard about."

Barb said, "It sounds odd, but when you think about it Christianity does have its roots in Judaism."

"Yes," replied Jim, "We're not going to get away from the Old Testament, are we?"

"No," said Barb, "we must begin with the Old Testament because that's really a part of our faith, it's our history too."

Pastor Bill said he would like to spend some time discussing the history of the United Methodist Church, so they could understand more about our local church. He said they would start by recognizing our Jewish background, then to the first 500 years of Christianity, the

Protestant Reformation, and finally discuss John and Charles Wesley and their influence on the United Methodist Church.

As we all know our Christian Churches began with Christ, but Jesus was a Jew, his disciples were Jews, and almost all of the early followers of Jesus were Jews. Christianity arose out of Judaism. That is one reason why our Bibles contain the Old Testament and we consider the Old Testament as Scripture. We have a common ancestry. The promises God made to the Jews he also made to us because we came from Judaism. The Jewish Scriptures, which are our Old Testament, depict a long history of dealing with God and we are a part of this sacred history. If the Old Testament is a history or compilation of books written about God and his dealings with His people, it is our history as well.

We remember Adam and Eve and their problems in the Garden of Eden. They ate of the fruit of the tree of knowledge of good and evil. As a result of this action they were put out of the Garden because they placed their wills over the will of God, and the infection of that prideful sin has come down to us today. This sin courses through all of humanity from one generation to the next. This sinful infection has come down to us as well because we are a part of that creation and fall. It wasn't just Eve, even though lied to by the snake or serpent she ate of it and it was good. It wasn't just Adam, because he also ate. It wasn't just the serpent even though he began it all. Eve told God she was lied to and she ate. Adam blamed Eve who God had given him, so he blamed both Eve and God.

"Girls, Just like a man," said Felista, "blame the woman and everyone else but himself."

"Harrumph," said James.

The story of Adam and Eve is our story as well because we follow the same path.

We can recall Abram whose name was changed by God to Abraham after his encounter with God. By faith he followed the will of God into a new land. He was told he would be the father of many nations and his descendents would be a light to the world. We are a part of this history as well.

We can recall Isaac, the only son of Abraham who was offered to God as a sacrifice, and then became the father of Jacob and Esau. We remember the problems of the sold birthright for a bowl of stew and the misplaced blessing given to Jacob rather than Esau because of the maneuvering of Jacob and his mother. We remember the reconciliation of Jacob and Esau many years later, despite Jacob's fears. All this history is ours also.

We can recall Joseph, the beloved of Jacob, and because of this, he was hated by his brothers. He was sold into slavery but he was also at the right place and time to help his family when they were in need because of the famine which Joseph had forewarned and prepared the Egyptians so they could live through those hard times. This is a part of our heritage.

Who can forget the giant religious leader of Israel, Moses, who was saved from the slaughter of the young Israeli boys by an Egyptian princess? He had to flee from Egypt because he could not bear to see the Jews misused and abused and he killed an Egyptian soldier. Moses met God in a bush which was burning but not consumed. From then until his death he was the leader of Israel who not only led his people out of Egypt but gave his people God's Ten Commandments. He led them for years but was not allowed to go into the land God promised the Jews and he died just before they entered. This is our history too.

We can recall the Psalms, the hymns and very personal dealings and discussions, pleadings, and prayers to God. There are songs of Thanksgiving and songs of lament. Almost anything we can experience in relationship to another or to God can be found in its pages.

We can recall Jonah and the big fish. The fish gets our attention but the real story is of a prophet of God who runs away from God so he does not have to preach to an enemy city because they might listen to God and change their ways. Then he is so upset because God causes a bush to grow up and shield him from the sun and then causes it to die. God asks why he is more concerned with the death of a plant than of a people. The story of Jonah is really the story of the Jewish people and their lack of missionary zeal. We are also a part of this.

And, who can forget the judges, kings and prophets of Israel? We remember Amos who gathered cheers when he talked about the sins of their neighbors and who, when he had them all listening, talked about the sins of Israel.

We remember Hosea who married a prostitute saying Israel had become a prostitute to other gods because they did not want to belong to the rightful and only God.

Remember the great one, Isaiah, who spoke so eloquently of the Suffering Servant. He wrote these familiar words:

> Who has believed what we have heard? And to whom has the arm of the Lord been revealed?
>
> For he grew up before him like a young plant,
>   and like a root out of dry ground:
> he had no form or majesty that we should look at him,
>   nothing in his appearance that we should desire him.
> He was despised and rejected by others;
>   a man of suffering and acquainted with infirmity;
> and as one from whom others hide their faces
>   he was despised, and we held him of no account.
>
> Surely he has born our infirmities and carried our diseases;
> yet we accounted him stricken—struck down by God, and afflicted.
> But he was wounded for our transgressions,
>   Crushed for our iniquities;
> Upon him was the punishment that made us whole,
>   And by his bruises we are healed.
> Isaiah 53:1-6

This too is a part of our common history.

The Hebrews have a long history of being found by God, selected by God, and then sharing a covenant with God.

Their story and ours is full of falling away from God and then repenting and returning to him only to fall away from him again. They discovered there was only one God and the rest were pretenders, idols made of wood, metal or other material, pretending to be God, but were really not gods at all. They, like us, either had God or an idol at the center of their lives. Humanity must have something at the center of his life and God says it should be him but sometime we push God out and put self-will, pride, and unbelief in God's place.

    "My goodness" Barb exclaimed; "I hadn't really put all this together. I wondered why my former pastor preached from the Old Testament and now I realize it is fully as much the Bible and up to date as our New Testament."

    "Yes," mused Felista, "I really liked to hear about these stories from the Old Testament, but I really didn't put them together as a part of our experience."

    Melissa spoke up "When I was a young girl I kind of had a crush on Sampson as he was portrayed in the movies."

    Shawn said, "I might like to read the Old Testament again as these stories have gotten me interested in them again."

    "Yes," said Todd, "hearing these brief stories about some of the events in the Old Testament got me interested in reading them again. I have read the Old Testament a couple of times and found the results to be mixed. I liked some of it but did not understand or like other parts."

B. First Five Hundred Years

    After a short break Pastor Bill said they were now going to look at the first 500 years of the Christian church because so much happened during this time which would put the church on the path it has taken ever since. They started as individuals or home churches with believers meeting together in small groups. Eye witnesses to part or all Jesus' entire ministry were still alive and they told others of the good news. Many were still around who witnessed the resurrection and could tell about it.

    Naturally all Christian churches began with Christ and with those immediate followers such as Peter, James the brother of Jesus, Paul, and the writers of the four gospels and Acts. They began to work out and explain what being a Christian entailed.

    During the early days of the Christian church a decision had to be made between being a sect or part of Judaism or whether the good news was taking us beyond a sect and to a new religion. St. Paul played a strong role in our becoming a new religion with his work with the Greeks and his insight into the uniqueness of Christianity. Even as Paul saw Christianity was something new and unique, he considered the Old Testament and its history of the Jews and God's dealing with them as Scripture and a part of the new good news. As we know the only Scripture the Jews had at the time was what we call the Old Testament.

One of the first big discussions was to determine whether Christianity which came from a Jew and a group of Jewish disciples, was to be a part of Judaism or whether Christianity was something entirely new. These early disciples or fathers in Christianity had to determine whether or not Greek or non-Jewish converts would have to be circumcised and conform to the religious laws and legal matters which the Jews did before becoming Christian, or if those who came to Christianity from outside Judaism were to be brought into the Christian church without having to participate in the Jewish rites first. In other words, do they have to become Jews first before they could be Christians and if so Christianity would really be a part of Judaism? If not, and converts would not have to become Jews first then Christianity was not a part of Judaism, but was an entirely new thing. We all remember the discussions Paul had and wrote about and it was eventually decided non-Jews would not have to be circumcised and we therefore had a new Church. Paul's idea was accepted by all of the key disciples.

The New Testament, which is the Word of God for us, contains the writings of many of the early Christians about their experiences with Jesus and their understanding of what God has done for us through him. The whole history of salvation is covered which culminated in the life, death, and resurrection of Jesus.

Following the death of Jesus and his early followers there were lots of discussions, indeed many arguments, about what Christians should believe and what writings should be included in the canon, which is the name given to those books which have been accepted, agreed to, and now are the books in our New Testament.

These arguments as to which writings should be accepted and which were not accepted took many years, prayerful study, and many discussions and shared thoughts, or meetings of the church to finally reach agreement. The church tended to accept the earliest writings which were often tied to or linked with some of the early disciples or followers of Jesus, and exclude those writings which were written much later. We think this was an excellent decision because some of the later writings were very different from the understanding and perspective of the earlier ones.

During the first 500 years the church also had several councils or meetings called Ecumenical, to determine what we as Christians are to believe, particularly about Jesus of Nazareth and the Holy Spirit. Probably many organizations go through a period of creation, clarification and adjustment. However, this was entirely different because lives were at stake and the relationship of God and humanity and eternal life were in the balance. This was not just the start and ordering of a new committee or club, this was the faithful trying to understand logically who and what was this Jesus and because of this, what changes are made for us. The church had many concepts put forward by men who thought they understood what it means to be a Christian and what we are to believe. It took many meetings of Christians for us to determine what the beliefs we had to hold were and what ideas and beliefs were to be excluded or condemned.

It took the Christian Church 500 years to settle the many different concepts of Christianity and which books were to be accepted and should be included in the New Testament. During these years various creeds were accepted such as the Apostle's Creed and the Nicene Creed. These creeds have come down to us today and are repeated in Christian churches throughout the world.

By common usage of the books and also by common consent, the books of the New Testament we have today were gradually brought together. Early on the letters of Paul were accepted probably because they were written closest in time to the life of Jesus and the impact of Paul on the early church. Then the four Gospels were pretty much accepted. Each book which was accepted meant some others were either not accepted yet or were rejected entirely. Sometime around 367 C.E. all of the books of the New Testament were pretty well agreed upon by the early church fathers.

The Church of Rome was the predominant church in early Christianity but soon it divided into the Eastern and Western churches. It was natural for the church at Rome to be the main church because it was the main city of the Roman Empire. Even so, there was a lot of diversity in the churches for some time.

Barb asked "How did the church decide or make sure all parts of theology or ideas about Christ we believe today were settled upon?"

Pastor Bill replied, "That is an excellent question so let's take some time now to discuss it a little further."

The church had councils which determined which are the correct beliefs or statements. The process began in the 300 C.E.'s and ended in the late 400's. It took the church over 100 years, from 325 until 451 C.E. to complete the statement of our understanding of Christ and the Holy Spirit and those persons or views which were not consistent with these decisions were called heretical and excluded from the Christian perspective. They decided on the humanity of Christ and then the divinity of Jesus and then they decided he was human and divine, fully both. Ideas and concepts which differed from these agreed upon views were found to be outside of Christian thought and were not acceptable views for Christians.

Though there were several councils held in the early Catholic Church we will consider only three of them because they were those which brought most of the results we look back to today.

The first Ecumenical Council was in Nicaea in 325 C.E. Emperor Constantine called the Council to try to bring unity to the Roman Catholic Church in its theology as well as trying to eliminate the disunity in the empire's religion. About three hundred bishops attended this council, most of them coming from the Eastern part of the empire. Because the Bishop of Rome, due to his age was unable to attend, he sent several representatives.

At this council were two main factions. Arius taught the Son has a beginning, because he is the first born of the Father so there was a time before he was created. God however, has no beginning and therefore the Son is not a part of God.

The main result of this council was the belief Jesus was divine. Believe it or not, there were those like Arius who did not believe Jesus was fully divine, but this council affirmed Jesus' divinity. By way of explaining his divinity they said Jesus was of the same, not similar substance, as the Father and he is eternal. Dismissed from Christian thought was the idea Jesus was similar in substance with the Father but not of the same substance as the Father. Also done away with was the idea there was a time before Jesus. This council produced the beginning of what we know today as the Nicene Creed. Though it was basically complete it took a few years for the creed to settle into the form we have today.

The second Ecumenical Council we will discuss is the one in Constantinople in 381 C.E. One group headed by Apollinarius thought two complete and contrasting natures could not exist in one person. He did not think it possible Jesus could be fully human and fully divine. Others thought Jesus had to be both and there was a good deal of struggling in how to say it correctly. This council determined the Holy Spirit is also eternal and of the same substance as the Father and the Son. Other thinkers had presented the idea the Holy Spirit was subordinate to one of the other two or both, but this council determined the Holy Spirit was not subordinate to the Father or the Son and therefore was on the same level as the Father and the Son.

The Fourth Ecumenical council was in Chalcedon in 421 C.E. Remember we are not discussing all of the councils but only those which fit in with our work. This council determined Jesus was wholly God and wholly human, largely through the efforts of Leo I or "Leo the Great." The very nature of the Christian faith was at stake.

How Jesus was related to God and humanity certainly had something to say about the essentials of the Christian movement. If Christ could not be shown to be divine, then there could be no redemption through him. If Christ was not human, then his suffering was all a sham and the ethical imperative was greatly weakened, if not entirely lost. In other words they set out the belief in what they and we today call the incarnation. As strange as it may sound to us today at each step of the way or process of defining the faith there were Christians who presented and believed in other concepts. For every item of belief the church accepted others were of necessity rejected and declared outside the Christian faith.

Pastor Bill said it was amazing to him that the church was able to settle all these controversies in the first 500 years. Once in awhile today we find echoes of some of the rejected concepts but it is hard to find one which the church has not faced before. In such a short time the main tenets of the Christian faith were agreed to and the canon of the New Testament was established. Jesus was both fully human and fully divine and the Holy Spirit was not a lesser deity but was equally God. We now have the Trinity as well as the Incarnation resolved, two huge and necessary concepts for Christianity.

Jim said, "What was the Incarnation again?"

Felista replied" It means Jesus was both fully human and fully divine. I can't understand it, but I kind of understand what it means."

"You are so right," said Shawn, "I know what it means, I just don't know how it can be, or how logically to put it together."

"I'm amazed at how many things were accomplished in the first 500 years. Makes you wonder if they left anything else for others to do," said Melinda.

Barb laughingly said, "It would take our congress much longer to work it out than the Church has done."

"I always wondered how the Scriptures came to be collected and what the canon meant," said Shawn with his usual smile.

Todd said "it is surprising to me how much work they were able to do before the printing press was even invented."

"Speaking of the conclusion of 500 years, it hasn't been as long but let's take a break and refresh our drinks," said Pastor Bill.

C. Protestant Reformation

The next great change to affect Christianity was the Protestant Reformation which began in the 16th century C.E. Though others were questioning and unhappy with the church for various reasons, it was Martin Luther who tacked up his 95 theses for discussion on the church door in Wittenberg and these questions sparked the process of what became known as the Protestant Reformation.

We will just make some generalizations about the Protestant Reformation, important as it was for the future of the Christian Church. It is necessary for us to realize at the time there was a movement for change and this movement worked out in different ways for the church. We are all aware or have probably heard of the Protestant Reformation, but many of us are unaware there was also a Catholic Reformation going on at the same time.

Melinda said pensively, "I was raised a Roman Catholic as a girl and I've heard about the Catholic Reformation."

"I wonder why it didn't all work out so the church didn't have to split," said Felista.

"Let's see if we can at least partially answer the question," said Pastor Bill.

Obviously these two Reformations had some differences in how they wanted to accomplish change and indeed what they wanted to change. The second generalization is the Catholic Reformation sought all change to be performed within the Roman Catholic Church. It wanted a thorough moral change both in the clergy and in the laity. It fought to bring to all Christians a greater intellectual understanding of the key Christian teachings, a renewed life of prayer, performance of services to their neighbors, and bring the gospel to all of humanity.

Many of these issues would be agreed to by the Protestant Reformation as well. In seeking these changes the Catholic Reformation did not however, want to make any changes in their doctrine, they merely wanted to find ways of clarifying them, and in all these reforms they saw no reason to change the status of the Pope.

In varying ways the parts of the Protestant Reformation broke with the Church of Rome. All of them rejected the authority of the Pope. Many were willing to retain the hierarchy without the Pope. Many were happy with the Apostle's and Nicene Creeds. All of them believed the Scriptures were the authority but they did not agree on the books to be called Scriptures, neither did they agree with the concept the Pope was the only one who could interpret the Scriptures in a way which would bind all Christians. Almost all kept the two sacraments of baptism and the Lord's Supper, and rejected the other five.

The third generalization is the Roman Catholic Reformation generally followed the heart of the Roman Empire and the Protestant Reformation gathered support from around the outskirts of the Roman Empire and beyond.

The fourth generalization is the Protestant Reformation generally came from the lower classes whereas the Roman Catholic Reformation generally came from the higher and better educated groups.

The basis upon which Luther founded the new way of thinking was justification by faith alone by grace alone, and this concept came from his own personal experience. He sought for the Word of God to be primary in the church so he naturally strongly believed in preaching. Luther promoted the idea of the priesthood of all believers and therefore he had a heavy emphasis upon education so those believers would know the Gospel. He wanted us to go back to the New Testament and to purge from the church all of the changes which he thought the Roman Catholic Church made to the New Testament faith and practice. Though he differed radically on some points with the Roman Catholic Church he did not think they were wrong in everything they had done.

You may have heard about others from the time in addition to Martin Luther. The most famous of them are perhaps John Calvin who wrote the "Institutes of the Christian Religion" and Huldreich Zwingli both in the Reformed part of the church. A close friend of Luther's was Philip Melanchthon. There were certainly many others but these are the best known. There were many supporters of each of these men.

Luther and the other reformers threw out some of the books which were included by the Roman Catholic Church as a part of their canon. Protestants today call these books the apocrypha. They were written between the Old Testament and the New Testament and the reformers did not think they were of the same value as the other books. Publishers of Protestant Bibles will often include the apocrypha because today there is much interest in reading and becoming familiar with these books as well as the official books. They are used as a study of the background to the New Testament.

Some other denominations and Churches have different numbers. The Jews, Protestants and some Catholics have the same number of Old Testament books.

D. John Wesley and Methodism

"Now we are finally getting to an area I like and have studied a lot," said Pastor Bill.

"Yes, this is where I really thought we would begin our studies," said Shawn. "I can see why we started where we did but my first thought was that we would start with Wesley."

Then in the 18th century came John Wesley from the Anglican Church or Church of England. The Anglican Church for various reasons, both political and religious, was set right between Protestantism and Roman Catholicism. Sometimes it has been called as Catholic a Protestant church or as Protestant a Catholic Church as is possible.

John and his brother Charles wanted to be yeast or leaven within the Church of England, to renew and revitalize it. It did not work out for them for a variety of reasons. It did not help that at the time many within the Church of England received their pulpits politically and consequently were not always properly educated or really cared much for the church. Others may have misunderstood the messages of the Wesley's or been bullied into their antagonism by others, including some of the Bishops.

For whatever reasons the Wesley's were basically shut out of the pulpits of the Church of England but they remained working for renewal, even going so far as to preach in the fields or other open places where they could preach to the masses of people who came to hear them and their message. To the credit of the Church of England the Wesley's were not put out of the church, even though they caused it some grief.

Interestingly enough Methodism received its name from the jeers of other students in Oxford. John had assumed leadership in a group which was started by Charles. The group was interested in systematic Bible study, group discipline in keeping a keen devotional life maintained, and attending communion frequently. This group also was interesting in studying the early Christian fathers. They were called among other things, The Holy Club, The Reforming Club, Bible Moths, Methodists, Supererogation Men, and Enthusiasts. However for some reason the name Methodist was the one that stuck. Though Wesley was not happy with the title he finally accepted it.

Eventually the Wesley's were able to purchase some places where they could preach indoors called preaching houses. Regardless of the few preaching places they were able to purchase they continued to preach outside or in the open air, by traveling the countryside to bring God's message to the people.

When Charles got married and had children he did not travel as much. He also wrote Christian poems and became the troubadour of the new movement, publishing book after book of poems, many of which were put to music and are still in The Methodist Hymnal.

John was an exciting genius as a theologian as well as organizer. As a theologian he brought together insights from various positions and somehow was able to meld them together with greater insight and meaning than these concepts had when they stood alone.

He was a scholar of the first rank and was very familiar with the early Church Fathers, telling his ministers they should read them. He wrote grammars in English, French, Greek, Hebrew and Latin. Even though he was familiar with the King James Version of the Bible he most frequently read the New Testament in the original Greek.

In order to handle the amount of people to preach to and then organize them, John allowed circuit riders, who were mainly laymen, to preach, as John directed. He created the classes and bands because he became aware just preaching to people would result in a lot of them eventually falling away from their initial enthusiasm.

They had annual conferences even then, which had a lot to do with making sure the circuit riders, most of whom were not trained clergy, kept their preaching compatible with the teaching of Wesley. Those who could not or would not do this were dismissed. One can read in Wesley's Works the outline and conclusions of their annual discussions on doctrines. Charles for a long time was in charge of checking the preaching of the circuit riders and then badgering John until he finally released them if they did not follow their orders or in some other way were unfit.

John believed the Methodists, those who had given the spiritual direction of their lives to him, wanted him to be their religious guide and he took this responsibility very seriously, strenuously guarding them from excesses in theology while at the same time teaching them about real and scriptural Christian living.

"We will be studying more of Wesley's theology later," Pastor Bill informed them.

Though unfortunately Wesley was not able, to any extent, to become the leaven for the Church of England he desired, he did some amazing things with his life.

Because of his preaching to the poor and his work for them such as educational facilities and homes for orphans, some give John and his movement credit for keeping England from having a revolution like the one France experienced.

He preached about 42,000 sermons, he and Charles published over 500 titles with the bulk of them coming from the pen of John. Many of these books were called the Christian Library because they were compilations from many Christian authors edited by John so the uneducated could read them and learn about Christianity from them. We also have today the multivolume sets of the Works, Journals, and Letters as well as his comments upon the New and Old Testaments and his two volume Standard Sermons.

The Standard Sermons and comments on the New Testament are still required reading and English Methodist Ministers must pass a test on them. In America we are not supposed to preach contrary to what is in them.

Wesley was against the American Revolution because he was against all wars and did not want England to engage in a war with America. He was one of the few who thought it was wrong, just as he was one of the few against the slave trade and worked hard to try to eradicate it from England. He did help to bring about the legal change which was made in England.

Turning from England to America, Methodism began as a lay movement. Wesley sent two of his lay preachers to America to help and two years later he sent two more. One of the men was Francis Asbury, who undoubtedly was the most important person in early American Methodism. His work in presenting the theology of the Wesley's, his understanding of the ministry, and his ability to organize here were greater than any others. Eventually some American lay persons became lay preachers here.

The first conference in America was in 1773 and was held in Philadelphia. There were ten who attended this conference and they aligned themselves with Wesley's leadership and because they were not trained clergy, they agreed not to administer the sacraments to their followers. The Methodists were supposed to receive their sacraments from the local Anglican parish no matter how far away. They sought discipline among the societies they started and wanted the same discipline for the lay preachers. They also instituted annual conferences, somewhat like those Wesley had in England.

The American Revolution brought troubling times for the Methodists. Some ministers did not support the Revolution and refused to bear arms. When the war was over Wesley recognized the changes in relationship between England and the United States and between Methodists in England and the situation in the United States. Obviously the Anglican or Church of England ministers were not very popular here and many of them went back to England after the war.

Wesley first ordained and then sent Thomas Coke to America to superintend the work here in combination with Francis Asbury. Wesley had ordained two other ministers who came to America with Coke, Richard Whatcoat and Thomas Vasey. These ordinations by Wesley changed church polity and ultimately led to the independence of Methodists in America.

December 1784 was the date of the famous Christmas Conference in Baltimore at Lovely Lane Chapel. They were organized as The Methodist Episcopal Church in America and the next year they published their first Discipline.

About the same time two other churches which had some Methodist or Wesleyan influences came into being. They were called the Church of the United Brethren in Christ and The Evangelical Association.

In the early 1800's a religious growth began and was nourished. There were revivals and camp meetings to bring people to repentance and to Christ and then the circuit riders and lay ministers worked to help them become a group or church. All three churches were organized to take advantage of their environment and they grew.

The organization of the Methodists directed by the Book of Discipline and its structures were uniquely able to take maximum advantage of the times.

Sunday Schools sprang up and they were a source of new members for the churches. People came to the Sunday School and then they might join the church. Today this is all changed. Only about one half of the church members attend Sunday Schools and most Sunday School members belong to the church already. One wishes we could change this and use the Sunday Schools to get new folks interested in the church today. Maybe we need to rethink how we offer Sunday Schools or what we study.

The Methodist Book Concern was set up and it began publishing all kinds of materials for the church.

All was not peaceful in the Methodist Church because conflict over race led to the creation of two African American Churches. Then a large group broke off because lay people were not represented in the leadership of the church. Then the slavery issue created yet another division. The Methodist Episcopal Church and the newly created The Methodist Episcopal Church, South, separated over the issue.

When the Civil War arose, it was very difficult for the Methodist Episcopal Church, South because they lost many pastors and members to the war. The other Methodist churches were not hit as hard and in fact they began to grow after the war.

These churches had two more issues to contend with which were very difficult for them. The first was the representation of the laity within the church. Some agreed to it and others resisted but they all finally agreed in 1932 that the laity should be accepted and represented in the organization of the church and its conferences.

The second issue was about women and whether they could be ordained and whether they could fill lay offices and be represented in the church.

Further issues arose before and after World War I. Theologically the times were in ferment. Liberal Protestant theology, which warred with fundamentalism, had pretty well won out. It had been dominant for some time but it was now beginning to be attacked by a revitalized fundamentalism which became known as neo-orthodoxy. All Methodist Churches as well as other denominations were caught up in this theological war.

In 1939 The Methodist Episcopal Church, The Methodist Protestant Church, and The Methodist Episcopal Church, South, joined to form The Methodist Church.

The next big event was in 1968 when Methodists and the Evangelical and United Brethren united and became known as the United Methodist Church.

Since then many of the earlier problems have been largely overcome. Women now fill positions in all areas of the church. The United Methodist Church has also tried to become a church community, open to all regardless of race or ethnic background and make available to them membership and participation in all levels and areas of service within the church.

Pastor Bill said, "This is not a complete history by any means but it is all we can cover at this time. If we are going to finish our work we will have to move on to other topics."

"The problems which the early Methodists in the U.S faced was a completely new concept for me. My mental picture was of men on horseback going around preaching," said Diane.

"I did not realize the problems Wesley had in England. I did not know he had such a hard time being accepted and that some of the things he did such as preaching outdoors and praying extemporaneously were considered bad," stated Melinda.

"I did not know the circuit riders or lay preachers in England were not always well received," Todd spoke up, "nor did I realize Wesley kept such close control over their preaching but it makes sense when you realize they were not trained for the ministry."

Jim said "this presentation and discussion is very helpful to me to understand how Methodism got to America from England and how the church here was related to John Wesley.

"I was surprised by the breaking off of so many churches" said Felista. "I knew some of the reasons were pretty volatile at the time but did not realize church people separated over such things back then."

"Let me tell you about my previous church," Barb responded. "When I was in high school some of the people liked our pastor and some didn't and our church lost many members over the whole discussion and fight. In the final analysis the District Superintendent and Bishop had their way. Interestingly enough, many of those who wanted the pastor to move left the church after the Bishop moved him anyway. Seemed mighty strange to me."

Melinda spoke up, "I know of a church which had a long history of those who liked the pastor sat on one side of the aisle and those who did not sat on the other side. Seems the church had a pastor long ago and then a faction arose to get rid of him and then the other group started to do what they could to get rid of the other group's pastor. Finally a pastor came and his wife sat on one side one Sunday and on the other side the next Sunday. That finally cured them and they quit doing it."

SCRIPTURE

Thus says God, the Lord,
>who created the heavens and stretched them out,
>who spread out the earth and what comes from it,
who gives breath to the people upon it,
>and spirit to those who walk in it;
I am the Lord, I have called you in righteousness.
>I have taken you by the hand and kept you;
I have given you as a covenant to the people,
>a light to the nations,
>to open the eyes that are blind,
to bring out the prisoners from the dungeon,
>from the prison those who sit in darkness.
I am the Lord, that is my name;
>my glory I give to no other,
>nor my praise to idols.
See, the former things have come to pass,
>and new things I now declare;
before they spring forth,
>I tell you of them.
(Isaiah 42:5-9)

PRAYER

Almighty God, Heavenly Father, we are bold to come before you this day and thank you for the mighty works you have performed on our behalf. We now are able to look at the history of your Son and his works in the world since his birth, life, death and resurrection, and give you thanks for all those who have gone on ahead.

Bless us as we study this day the history of the Jews and Christians through the years. Your Kingdom comes near and is marching on to glory.

We thank you for all you have done for us, those things we recognize and those we do not or so easily forget.

We ask all this in the name of our Lord, Your Son, Jesus the Christ. Amen.

CHAPTER 3. QUESTIONS

1. Why did we start our study with the Jews and not Christians?

2. Are we a sect of Judaism or are we of a different faith? Discuss your reasons.

3. How did Christians work through our beliefs or belief system? Or, what methods did we use to put our thoughts together?

4. Discuss the work of the first, second and fourth ecumenical councils.

5. What was the Protestant Reformation?

6. Who are some of the Protestant Reformers and what were they known for?

7. Why did John and Charles Wesley want to start a new church?

8. What did John do to help preach the word of God when he could not handle it all?

9. The United Methodist Church has had many names. What are some of them and how did they come about?

CHAPTER 4 Methodist Beliefs

As they gathered for the next class Barb said laughingly, "I'm certainly glad to be dealing with the easy part of our studies now. This section really went way over my head and I had to read it several times."

"It certainly is not an easy concept," said Felista.

Todd spoke up, "I knew this area was coming so I got a book, "John Wesley, Natural Man, and the Isms"[3] and it explained some of the differences between Methodism and some other denominations and such. It was a little difficult but I got a lot out of it."

"It really isn't easy," said Diane, "I was about ready to pull my beautiful blonde hair out," she said laughingly, "I thought I was the only one having trouble with some of these concepts. It's nice to hear some of the rest of you are finding it difficult to pull together."

"We'll just have to wait for Pastor Bill to put it together for us," said Melinda, and they all laughed.

"Well," said Pastor Bill, "you have certainly given me a real challenge."

After the protestant and Roman Catholic reformations things were pretty quiet in the church, at least there were no more reformations. Then in the 18th century John and Charles Wesley arise and begin their efforts at reviving the Church of England which we discussed earlier.

Wesley took the 39 Articles of Religion of the Church of England and pared them down to 25 which he sent to America and are now found in our book of Discipline. The church in America is supposed to follow Wesley's Notes on the New Testament and the Standard Sermons. At least we are not to preach anything which is contrary to what is found in the Notes and the Standard Sermons.

When the churches joined in 1968, the Evangelical United Brethren Church had its own Articles of Religion which are also in our Discipline, but we will only consider the first group because to do both would be too lengthy and in fact they are very similar.

The first four Articles we will study have to do with our understanding or concept of God.

---

[3] Ewbank, J. Robert, *John Wesley, Natural Man, and the Isms*

Article I—Of Faith in the Holy Trinity

There is but one living and true God, everlasting, without body or parts, of infinite power, wisdom, and goodness; the maker and preserver of all things, both visible and invisible. And in unity of this Godhead there are three persons, of one substance, power, and eternity-the Father, the Son, and the Holy Ghost.[4]

Article II—Of the Word, or Son of God, Who Was Made Very Man

The Son, who is the Word of the Father, the very and eternal God, of one substance with the Father, took man's nature in the womb of the blessed Virgin; so that two whole and perfect natures, that is to say, the Godhead and Manhood, were joined together in one person, never to be divided; whereof is one Christ, very God and very Man, who truly suffered, was crucified, dead, and buried, to reconcile his Father to us, and to be a sacrifice, not only for original guilt, but also for actual sins of men.[5]

Article III—Of the Resurrection of Christ

Christ did truly rise again from the dead, and took again his body, with all things appertaining to the perfection of man's nature, wherewith he ascended into heaven, and there sitteth until he return to judge all men at the last day.[6]

Article IV—Of the Holy Ghost

The Holy Ghost, proceeding from the Father and the Son, is of one substance, majesty, and glory with the Father and the Son, very and eternal God.[7]

These four articles really tell us a lot about God, all in fact that is necessary for us to believe about him.

A. Trinity

It is easier for us to talk about the Father, or the Son, or the Holy Spirit, than it is to talk about the Trinity. Wesley had no trouble thinking of God as a Trinity but he knew some had problems with this designation. Because of this problem Wesley called God the Three-One for lack of a better description.

---

[4] *The Book of Discipline of the United Methodist Church*, 63-64
[5] Ibid, 64
[6] Ibid, 64
[7] Ibid, 64

Wesley said there are three on earth who testify to Jesus as the Christ and they are the Holy Spirit, the water which signifies we are dedicated to the Son, and the blood he shed which signifies the Lord's Supper.

There is another grouping of three, but they are in heaven, who testifies—the Father, the Word, and the Spirit. Wesley explains this passage in his Notes on the New Testament in this way:

> *And there are three that testify in heaven*—The testimony of the Spirit, the water, and the blood is by an eminent gradation corroborated by three who give a still greater testimony. *The Father*—Who clearly testified of the Son, both at His baptism and at His transfiguration. *The Word*—Who testified of Himself on many occasions, while He was on earth; and again, with still greater solemnity, after His ascension into heaven. *And the Spirit*—Whose testimony was added chiefly after His glorification....*And these three are one*—Even as those two, the Father and the Son, are one...Nothing can separate the Spirit from the Father and the Son. If He were not one with the Father and the Son, the apostle ought to have said, *The Father and the Word*, who are one, *and the Spirit, are two*. But this is contrary to the whole tenor of revelation. It remains that *these three are one*. They are one in essence, in knowledge, in will, and in their testimony.[8]

You see the word Trinity is not in the Bible, there is no place in the Scriptures which tells us there is a Trinity and who composes the Trinity. However, there are many passages in the Scriptures which lead

---

[8] Wesley, John, *Notes on the New Testament*, 917-18

us to the conclusion all three are God and God is all three. Jesus himself talked about God, and the Father, and the Spirit.

One way Christians have tried to describe it in a type of theological formula is to say the Father is not the Son or the Holy Spirit; the Son is not the Father or the Holy Spirit; and the Holy Spirit is not the Father or the Son. However, the Father is God, the Son is God and the Holy Spirit is God. You may have seen this diagramed somewhere because it is a common explanation used to help us grasp the idea.

Pastor Bill tried to help by pointing out it may be easier to think of it the way Wesley described it. We know the fact of the Three-One God, but the manner of how this is and how it works is beyond our human comprehension. We know it and can understand it in part but thank goodness God does not require us to know how it works because he has not revealed this information to us in the Scriptures.

God has revealed to us that he is Three-One but he has not revealed to us how this apparent contradiction can exist. This answer is beyond our ability to understand and since God has not revealed it to us we do not know and are not responsible before him to know it.

Our view of the Trinity is not much different from any other mainline Christian church. We all believe in the Trinity and in the oneness of God.

Think about it this way. We have all experienced the Three-One God or we would not be here. We know what the Son has done for us because we have read the Scriptures and listened to many sermons. We all know what the Father has done for us because from his love for us he sent the Son. And, if we believe in Jesus it is the work of the Holy Spirit within us. Since Jesus is no longer here among us and said he would send the Spirit, it is through the Spirit we know of Jesus or the Father. The Spirit points and leads us to both. So in this way we can all say we are familiar with and have experience with the Three-One God.

Jim told Pastor Bill "The Trinity is a pretty complex proposition and thank goodness you do not have to know all the answers to it. I hope not all Methodist beliefs will be so complex and difficult to understand."

Pastor Bill said "This particular area is complex and we will have one other discussion which is complex but most of the rest certainly will not be so difficult."

Melinda cheerfully said "I'm thankful that's true."

"I have heard about the Trinity for years," said Diane, "but did not know how it could mean three persons were one. It is a difficult thing to understand. Thank goodness I don't or we don't have to fully understand it."

"You know you're right," replied Todd, "if you are a Christian you have experienced the Trinity. I just never did think of it that way."

"Yeah, this helped me too," said Shawn.

Felista joined in, "our former pastor talked about all three but did not put them together like this. It makes better sense to me now."

Jim and Barb agreed they had heard of the Trinity when they were in church as teenagers but they really did not comprehend the uniqueness and difficulty of understanding it.

B. Jesus, Son of God

After a short break to refresh them and get ready for a new topic Pastor Bill began by saying, "Jesus is the Son of God."

Jesus was a human being who lived among us. He was human just like we are. When he itched he scratched and when his skin was pierced he bled. Jesus got hungry and he was thirsty, and he was tired, all just like we are because he was the physical and human son of Mary. This is wonderful for us because we know Jesus is aware of all the fears and pains we face as human beings because he has lived through them.

His ministry was spent in a small area in a pretty insignificant but rebellious little group of cities at the edge of the Roman Empire. He was baptized by his cousin John, preached to those who followed him, talking a lot about the Kingdom of God and its closeness to humanity. He worked with his disciples to help them understand him, his ministry, and the God he revealed.

In fact we know precious little about his youth or teen years. The Gospels and writers about Jesus were focused more on what he had done than they were about his early life, probably which was spent learning his father's trade and working with him and later as at least one of the breadwinners. Since Joseph is not mentioned other than when Jesus was born and shortly thereafter such as taking Jesus to the temple, we assume he died while Jesus was young but not before some other children were born such as James.

His ministry lasted about three years and began when he was baptized by John and ended on a cross. The gospels tell us a lot about those three years, each from their own perspective and for the audience to which they were writing.

Jesus had conflicts with some as he preached his message because his message was of God and God's kingdom and was therefore not always in agreement with the established order. The Jewish leaders were always trying to keep from attracting the attention of Rome and also trying to keep faith with their temple, its priests, and whole religious system.

For whatever the reason or reasons, political and/or religious, he came to the attention of the Jewish leaders and they caught him, tried him, turned him over to the Romans who whipped him and eventually crucified him as a common criminal. The only interest he would have received from the Romans was if they thought he would be a problem in keeping the peace.

His message was about the kingdom of God which he said was coming and even present in part in him and his works, and in the life and work of his disciples. God was making himself known and his kingdom was even then breaking into history.

John baptized but Jesus did not. He was baptized by John but his ministry was one of believing in him and having faith in God's works through him. If he had been much of a disciple of John as some would have us believe he surely would have baptized people as John predominantly did, but he did not do so.

However Jesus was not only wholly human, he was also wholly divine. All our creeds point to this fact. As Wesley said earlier, this is the fact but the manner of how God did it is not known to us and indeed is not revealed to us. Since the manner of how God performed his work has not been revealed to us we do not have to know how it was done; only that it was done.

In the early days of the church there was a lot of discussion about Jesus and some in the discussion thought he was not divine but only human. Such a belief would have Jesus as a good person, maybe the best person who ever lived, but this thought would probably result in our making an ethic out of Christianity by following his ethical teachings, not a religion. This particular concept of Jesus was decided to be error and in the first five centuries of the Church was labeled out of bounds for the Christian Church.

Others in the church took the opposite view and said he was divine and only appeared to be human. They considered humanity as evil and sinful and there was no way therefore God could be human. Jesus' humanity was a sham because he was totally divine and only seemed as if he was human. This idea was likewise put outside the bounds of Christian thought and was regarded as heresy. It did not fit with what we know and believe.

The concept which was finally accepted was Jesus was wholly human and yet wholly God. Somehow he was both and fully both. Though we don't know how Jesus could be both because our finite minds cannot fathom this truth, this is our truth.

In a letter to a Roman Catholic Wesley presents what he and we believe:

> I believe that Jesus of Nazareth was the Saviour of the world, the Messiah so long foretold; that, being anointed with the Holy Ghost, He was a Prophet, revealing to us the whole will of God; that He was a Priest, who gave Himself a sacrifice for sin, and still makes intercession for transgressors; that He is a King, who has all power in heaven and in earth, and will reign till He has subdued all things to Himself.
>
> I believe He is the proper, natural Son of God, God of God, very God of very God; and that He is the Lord of all, having absolute, supreme, universal dominion over all things; but more peculiarly our Lord, who believe in Him, both by conquest, purchase, and voluntary obligation.
>
> I believe He was made man, joining the human nature with the divine in one person; being conceived by the singular operation of the Holy Ghost, and born of the blessed Virgin Mary…[9]

Some folks would tell us that outside of the Bible, which they don't believe in, there is no evidence Jesus ever lived. This is an

---

[9] Wesley, *Letters*, 3:8-9

interesting thought but there is as much evidence, truly more, that he lived than many others who we believe lived during that time and not all the evidence comes from the New Testament alone. Since we have no problem believing some of these other people existed with less evidence for them than we have Jesus existed, we should be able to believe in the existence of Jesus.

If Jesus did not exist where in the world would the entire New Testament come from? There are several authors of all these books. Did they all get together over many years which span the writing time for these books and somewhere agree to write about this fictitious character? Did they, though at different locations as well as different times, all agree to write about this person as if he existed and somehow kept secret their writings were false so people would believe in him and die rather than recant their faith? Can we by any stretch of the mind believe such a fairy tale? No, we can't because it is just not true. There are also many books written about Jesus which were not included or accepted by the church and yet we are supposed to believe all these writings written about this person who did not exist when the authors seemed to believe it? It strains our credulity to believe this could ever happen. And, then, to have people for two centuries believe these lies to the detriment of their lives and their religious life, and yet no one can prove he did not exist?

"When you put it that way it's hard to see how so many don't believe in Jesus. I've never thought of it in that manner," said Diane.

Melinda said, "I've never thought of it this way but I have wondered at times about Jesus and what he did and if we really could believe it. Now, with what we have discussed I understand it much better"

"I really appreciated this part of the study," said Shawn and Todd nodded his agreement.

Jim agreed and said "I am happy we now have gotten by all of the difficult areas," and the others laughed.

C. Resurrection

There are those also who think Jesus was not raised from the dead. Some say he was not really dead when he was taken down from the cross regardless of the fact he was whipped and on the cross for several hours and men did not live on the cross very long. Somehow, the soldiers did not know he was alive though perhaps comatose so they let him be taken away to be buried, when in fact they broke the legs of the others because they knew they were still alive?

Others try to explain what happened by saying the disciples crept into the crypt and took Jesus' body away, hid, and buried it at another location. Then they declared he had risen. What a thought this is for us. This way of thinking would require so many lies told by so many people for so long, and yet none of them slipped and told another person the whole thing was a sham, a lie, and how they were able to fool everybody?

The Roman soldiers had to make sure all of the men on the crosses every day were dead before they would allow them to be taken down and moved. Did the Roman soldiers never see a dead person before, so they would not know one was alive? How many would they let live before they were in trouble? No, we can't believe in this. Wouldn't Rome and especially the Jews be happy to report these were all lies and nothing like the resurrection happened? It would be in their best interests to say so.

We have in Scripture many witnesses to the resurrection who could have been and probably were questioned by others as to the true facts. Anyone could ask many of them. Even as late as Paul's time he says there were several still alive and they could witness to the resurrection. Are all these people lying? Did they all get together to perpetrate this lie without anybody among the group letting any of this lie slip? Can we believe in such a thing when we all have experiences of telling a friend a secret only to have it very quickly get out to many others? On top of this when we tell a friend a secret it gets twisted soon and the resulting story may or may not resemble the start.

One of the Wesley hymns says it so well about what we believe in Christ

> Jesus, my Lord, attend
> Thy fallen creature's cry,
> And show Thyself the sinner's Friend,
> And set me up on high:
> From hell's oppressive power,
> From earth and sin release,
> And to Thy Father's grace restore,
> And to Thy perfect peace.

> For this, alas! I mourn
> In helpless unbelief,
> But Thou my wretched heart canst turn,
> And heal my sin and grief;
> Salvation in Thy name
> To dying souls is given,
> And all may, through Thy merit, claim
> A right to life and heaven.
>
> Thy blood and righteousness
> I make my only plea,
> My present and eternal peace
> Are both derived from Thee:
> Rivers of life Divine
> From Thee their Fountain flow,
> And all who know that love of Thine
> The joy of angels know.
>
> O then impute, impart
> To me Thy righteousness,
> And let me taste how good Thou art,
> How full of truth and grace:
> That Thou canst here forgive
> I long to testify,
> And justified by faith to live,
> And in that faith to die.[10]

Melinda said "I did not realize there were those who thought the resurrection was just a story the apostles dreamed up. I did know some people did not believe in the resurrection but did not realize some of them actually thought the apostles and others dreamed up the charade of the resurrection."

"Wow," replied Todd, "this was new to me. I knew some people didn't believe in the resurrection but I didn't know they looked at it this way."

Barb said "The presentation really answered my questions about how somebody or a group of people could tell a lie of this

---

[10] Burtner, Robert and Chiles, Robert, *A Compend of Wesley's Theology*, 86-87

magnitude and no one ever slip. You really have to believe in the resurrection or you have to figure out how all these people could propagate a lie."

"I really appreciated going through this," responded Felista," it helps me understand the whole area."

"Yes," said James, "I certainly agree."

D. Holy Spirit

The third member of the Trinity, the Holy Spirit or Holy Ghost, is often given less attention than the other two, yet for us in the Christian life, he is extremely important.

The workings of God in our lives are all performed through the activity of the Holy Spirit. It is the Holy Spirit who calls us, who works in us, prepares us to even think about God, and about wanting to be closer to him.

The Holy Spirit convinces us we are separated from God, we have tried to get along by what we think of are our own devices—our strength, our knowledge, our insight, our foresight—not recognizing all of these thoughts or yearnings really come from God, the Holy Spirit.

We find the Holy Spirit mentioned in the New Testament. Jesus promised the Holy Spirit would come. Towards the end of his ministry he was facing death and the time he would be with his disciples was coming to an end. The Gospel of John has the story of the Holy Spirit. Jesus said he would not leave his followers alone in the world. Jesus could not remain with his disciples but the Counselor, the Holy Spirit, could be with all of his followers at every place where they were—who other than God could do this?

When Pentecost came the promise of Jesus that he would send the Holy Spirit was fulfilled in spades. Think of it, the disciples were fearful because Jesus had been crucified, Judas was dead, they did not know if the authorities were coming for them, and they did not know what they were going to do. In an upper room they had gathered to pray remembering the words of the Master that they would receive power when the Holy Spirit came to them. Then, the Holy Spirit did come.

Just think, Simon Peter who was afraid to admit he was a follower of Jesus to a maid only a few days before, could now stand and face the people of Jerusalem and deliver a powerful sermon about his risen Lord. Even though the same people and power structure were there who put Jesus on the cross, he was emboldened enough to speak out and many became followers of the way when he had finished. This has been the wonder of Christian history, what people could not do alone they could do with the power of the Holy Spirit. In the Scriptures there is a lot of discussion about the Holy Spirit, but even so the disciples were surprised by what they could receive from him.

The Holy Spirit is God within us, working in us and ever pulling and urging us to grow in our relationship with God and our fellowship and desire to serve the needs of our fellow humans.

The Holy Spirit is God within us telling us when we have sinned, we should not have performed this deed or thought, and leading us to accept the free grace which God would give us. The Holy Spirit is not apart from the other two of the Trinity as we have seen; therefore he is the presence of the living Christ in us. So, to put it another way, the Holy Spirit is the unseen God within us ever working to help us grow more loving of him and our fellow humans.

The Holy Spirit uses our conscience to daily instruct us about those things we should and shouldn't do. We may try to put ourselves forward for the abilities we have, the opportunities we have taken regardless of our worthiness etc… and then the Holy Spirit reminds us we are human and therefore sinful when we put ourselves at the center of the universe and our wants and wishes become our supreme command.

In our daily lives we can know the Holy Spirit by the way we feel pulled to help, to do, and yes, even to avoid. It is God speaking to us with the language of love.

The Holy Spirit wants to help us grow in the Christian life. He exposes to us our sin and separation from God and he shows us how to open our lives more fully to receive God so we can be the light which is not hidden and the salt of the earth which has not lost its saltiness. Through prayers, reading Scripture, study classes, being with and learning from other Christians who are further along in the growth of Christian living, we can learn more about and receive the encouragement of God's love for our lives.

As Wesley says:
> The author of faith and salvation is God alone. It is he that works in us both to will and to do. He is the sole Giver of every good gift, and the sole Author of every good work. There is no more of power than of

> merit in man; but as all merit is in the Son of God, in what he has done and suffered for us, so all power is in the Spirit of God. And therefore every man, in order to believe unto salvation, must receive the Holy Ghost. This is essentially necessary to every Christian, not in order to his working miracles, but in order to faith, peace, joy, and love,— the ordinary fruits of the Spirit.
>
> Although no man on earth can explain the particular manner wherein the Spirit of God works on the soul, yet whosoever has these fruits, cannot but know and feel *that* God has wrought them in his heart.
>
> Sometimes He acts more particularly on the understanding, opening or enlightening it, (as the Scripture speaks,) and revealing, unveiling, discovering to us "the deep things of God."
>
> Sometimes He acts on the wills and affections of men; withdrawing them from evil, inclining them to good, inspiring (breathing, as it were) good thoughts into them…[11]

The Holy Spirit speaks to us in many ways, one of which is assurance. We are assured we are children of God when we speak to God through prayer. Not only does the Holy Spirit witness to us we are children of God, if we are truly his children, our lives will begin to show the fruits of the Spirit.

What are these fruits? The fruits of the spirit, the things which we begin to see in our lives we did not see before are love, joy, peace, patience, kindness, goodness, faithfulness, gentleness, and self-control which were not as evident in our lives before. They may and probably

---

[11] Wesley, *Works*, 8:49

will not come full blown into our lives but we will begin to see growing evidence they are there.

The fruits of the spirit are not self-created. These fruits are the gift of God and come to us through the work of the Holy Spirit. We Methodists are not alone in our perception of the power of the Spirit's fruits as coming not from ourselves but from God. Try as we might, we are not able to create these fruits; they come not from our efforts but from the work of the Holy Spirit within us.

The Scriptures have warned us of the seven deadly sins (greed, sloth, lust, gluttony, anger, envy, and pride). Unfortunately in our topsy-turvy world some of us have made of them the good life, the life we should all be seeking and enjoy. These are not the good life, neither are they the way things should be, they really are the seven deadly sins and not fruits of the Spirit. Life can be enjoying the seven deadly sins or the fruits of the Spirit and each of us has to choose which way we will live our lives.

How can a sinner know
  His sins on earth forgiven?
How can my gracious savior show
  My name inscribed in heaven?
What we have felt and seen,
  With confidence we tell;
And publish to the sons of men,
  The signs infallible.

We who in Christ believe
  That he for us hath died.
We all his unknown peace receive,
  And feel his blood applied'
Exults our rising soul,
  Disburden'd of her load,
And swells unutterly full
  Of glory and of God.

> We by his Spirit prove
>   And know the things of God,
> The things which freely of his love
>   He hath on us bestow'd
> His Spirit to us he gave,
>   And dwells in us, we know:
> The witness in ourselves we have,
>   And all its fruits we show.[12]

"I know God is everywhere and in us but I did not know He was there as the Holy Spirit," said Shawn. "I never thought of God as being the Holy Spirit in me."

Barb said "I read somewhere God was within, and without, he was to our right and left and was with us forever and if this is true we know him because he is within us."

Felista said, "I like the Holy Spirit and believe he is present in me and at times I feel closer to him than others. I have seen others who have felt his closeness, too."

Melinda pondered, "Do you suppose that voice I hear in my mind sometimes might be God speaking to me?"

"No," Todd replied, "that's just you wanting to do what you want to."

Everyone laughed and then Barb said she thought what Melinda had said was right.

Pastor Bill said he would like to say a few words about God as Father. In calling God Father, we are saying God is like a good father. Unfortunately not everyone has a loving father so they may have a difficult time of thinking about God as Father, because their experiences with their own father was unloving, unconcerned, and sometimes abusive or totally absent.

Jesus came to tell us about God and God's desire for our lives. The Father he points to is one of love, of peace, of understanding. This Father can accept us and love us just as we are, warts and all. We don't have to try to fool him by wearing one of our "nice" masks; God knows who we are anyway and he loves us regardless.

"God so loved the world," he really does love us and wants what is best for us. He loves us even when we sin—"God so loved the

---

[12] Wesley, *Hymns*, 96 vs. 1,2,4

world." Before Jesus came to us and because it was necessary for him to come, it shows the unbelievable, wonderful, creative, love of God for us.

If He did not love us he would not have sent the Son into the world to show us what kind of God he is. He accepts and forgives us just as we are. We don't have to earn his love, we can't, because it is freely given to us.

Christ did for us not so we could learn how to be good but so our sins could be forgiven. God performed this mighty work not for the angels but for us and he freely wants to share this love. All we have to do is accept his love and our lives will be forever changed.

Do you have a hard time accepting gifts from others? Do you work at a feverish pace to make others happy and have them love you? Are you unable to say "no" to any request from others? If so you probably do not think others will really like you if they really got to know the real you. This is a lie from our enemy. God knows you, the real and total you and he loves you still. He sent the Son into the world for you and countless others like you. God thinks you are worthy of his love, why don't you?

Margot Starbuck writes in her book, "Not Who I Imagined" which is a study about who God really is:

> Like Don, we've been reluctant to look into our own hearts to notice what type of God we've come to believe. If we're religious, the dissonance between what we publicly profess—namely, God's benevolence—and what we secretly hold in our hearts, God's judgment, can feel frightening. So we continue to tout the party line about God's goodness even as we fail to experience God's graciousness deep within ourselves.[13]

Though we may not have perfect fathers, can we not understand and believe God loves us, even us, just as we are? He knows all our secrets, poses, fears, uncertainties, misbeliefs, sins, and

---

[13] Starbuck, Margot, *Not Who I Imagined*, 27

everything else and he still loves us and wants the best for us. He says nothing in the world or out of the world can separate us from his love.

You see we tend to look at God in a certain way because of our past experiences, but this way of looking may be incorrect. As Nicholas Sparks writes in his book about how some adult children may incorrectly look at their mother:

> Part of their error, she knew, stemmed from their desire to see her in a certain way, a preformed image they found acceptable for a woman her age. It was easier—and frankly more comfortable—to think their mom was more sedate than daring, more of a plodder than someone with experiences that would surprise them. And in keeping with the kind, predictable, sweet, and stable mother that she was, she'd had no desire to change their minds.[14]

What a marvelous father, full of love, who wants nothing more than our return of his love, who has done so much for us.

"Ah me," said Diane, "that really is helpful to me. My father was not the best and then he up and left us."

"Oh, I'm so sorry," said Barb, "I didn't know that. It must have been very difficult for you."

"Well," Diane haltingly replied, "I usually just say it was all right but this talk about God as Father and what kind of Father he is brought these old memories back. I'm happy to really know God as Father is different from mine. Oh my, I didn't mean for my eyes to water like this." She was given a big hug by Barb, Melinda and Felista.

---

[14] Sparks, Nicholas, *Nights in Rodanthe*, 10

SCRIPTURE

In the beginning was the Word, and the Word was with God, and the Word was God. He was in the beginning with God. All things came into being through him, and without him not one thing came into being. What has come into being in him was life, and the life was the light of all people. The light shines in the darkness, and the darkness did not overcome it. (John 1:1-5)

PRAYER

Father God, Creator of all and Redeemer of your fallen creation, we give you thanks for your revealing of yourself through the Scriptures but especially through your Son, Jesus our Christ who came into the world, lived in the world to teach and instruct us, and who died upon a cross for our sins and was raised from the dead on the third day.

We look at ourselves and find we are sinful, we are not holy, we are not just, we are not righteous, we are turned inwards towards ourselves, but into this darkness has come your light and we are thankful.

Be with and bless us this day as we begin the studies of those things we believe. Help us to understand and appreciate your revealing of yourself because we could not seek and find without your help and love.

We ask all these things in the name of Christ. Amen.

CHAPTER 4. QUESTIONS

1. Can we rationally explain the Trinity? Why not?

2. How would you explain the Trinity to someone who had no familiarity with Christianity?

3. Was Jesus a human being? Was Jesus God?

4. How do you reconcile Jesus as a human and Jesus as God?

5. Some people do not believe in the existence of such a person as Jesus. How would you answer them?

6. Some people do not believe Jesus was resurrected and it was just a big scam. How would you answer them?

7. Jesus said he would send the Holy Spirit. What is the Holy Spirit's job or what does he do on earth?

8. What are the fruits of the Spirit?

9. Are "the seven deadly sins" deadly, or are they the normal way of living?

CHAPTER 5 Methodist Beliefs (cont.)

Article VII—Of Original or Birth Sin

Original sin standeth not in the following of Adam (as the Pelagians do vainly talk), but it is the corruption of the nature of every man, that naturally is engendered of the offspring of Adam, whereby man is very far gone from original righteousness, and of his own nature inclined to evil, and that continually.[15]

"Ask Barb about original sin," laughed Jim. "She seems to think at times I've found it and practice it regularly."

"That's not true," said Barb. "What I talk about has nothing to do with original sin—forgetfulness, lack of concern sometimes, and often just plain unaware of what needs to be done."

"I can relate to that," said Melinda. "Todd forgets to help sometimes, however I'd rather have him forgetting sometimes than not remembering at all."

"Girls," said Felista. "They all have something missing because they can walk right by work that obviously needs to be done and never see it. I don't know if it is in their genes or if their mother's couldn't get the proper work done with them."

"I think it is time to remain silent," said Shawn, and Todd just quietly nodded his head in agreement.

Then Todd said, "Hey I finished a chapter in a book "Wesley's Wars[16]" on original sin and it was very interesting and informative. I did not realize how basic the concept of sin is for Christianity."

Just then Pastor Bill entered the room and the good natured comments ceased. Pastor Bill said he would talk about original sin and free will today.

Original sin goes to the heart of the matter of our understanding about humanity. We must take our understanding about ourselves and our condition before God seriously, because if we don't we need go no further because God can do nothing for you if you find no need for him.

If you believe there is a God is he so far removed from you and your life that his existence makes no change in your thinking or behavior? If this is the case I suggest your God is powerless and

---

[15] *The Book of Discipline of the United Methodist Church*, 65, 2012
[16] Ewbank, J. Robert, *Wesley's Wars*

certainly does not make a difference in this world or possibly the next and does not particularly care about you. You have a god but your god is not the Christian God.

Do you see or believe humanity is getting better day by day? Is humanity doing fine by itself and therefore does not need the help of anyone else to live life to the fullest? Or do you see or believe humanity needs help because somehow we are twisted and broken when we are living apart from God? Does your newspaper, like mine, carry stories every day of our brokenness and showing our evil nature? Are we able to love our neighbor and God without God's help?

"As a Christian," Pastor Bill explained, "we believe humanity simply cannot go it alone. We can try but when we do we get in trouble, are alienated from our true purposes, and cannot receive the happiness and joy we were meant to have."

There are several descriptions of humanity but one of the more satisfying is we were made to give allegiance to something, to follow something in order for it to make sense. The Scriptures tell us we were made in the image of God and we are to reflect the image but we can't do it without help. The image we are to reflect has become twisted, distorted, and the part expressing the relationship between us and God is entirely gone.

Wesley expressed it this way:

> "And God," the three-one God, "said, Let us make man in our image, after our likeness. So God created man in his own image, in the image of God created he him:" (Gen. i. 26,27)—Not barely in his *natural image*, a picture of his own immortality; a spiritual being, endued with understanding, freedom of will, and various affections;—nor merely in his *political image*, the governor of this lower world, having "dominion over the fishes of the sea, and over all the earth;"—but chiefly in his *moral image*; which, according to the Apostle, is "righteousness and true holiness." (Eph. iv.24) In this image of God was man made. "God is love:" Accordingly, man at his creation was full of love;

> which was the sole principle of all his tempers, thoughts, words, and actions. God is full of justice, mercy, and truth; so was man as he came from the hands of the Creator. God is spotless purity; and so man was in the beginning pure from every sinful blot; otherwise God could not have pronounced him, as well as all the other work of his hands, "very good." (Gen. i. 31.) And this he could not have been, had he not been pure from sin, and filled with righteousness and true holiness. For there is no medium: If we suppose an intelligent creature not to love God, not to be righteous and holy, we necessarily suppose him not to be good at all; much less to be "very good."
>
> But, although man was made in the image of God, yet he was not made immutable. This would have been inconsistent with that state of trial in which God was pleased to place him. He was therefore created able to stand, and yet liable to fall. This God himself apprized him of, and gave him a solemn warning against it. Nevertheless, man did not abide in honour: He fell from his high estate.[17]

So, we can either give our life to God or we will give it to sins of one type or another—self-will, pride, and unbelief.

Wesley likened our condition to a disease which travels down from one generation to another. We are sinful creatures, full of pride, self-will, and unbelief, and by our own power we cannot fix our

---

[17] Wesley, *Works*, 6:66-67

brokenness. Like Humpty Dumpty we are unable to put ourselves back together again.

True, we can do many good things; but we are talking about our creation and our need for God if we are to be as God created us to be. We obviously are now apart from God, not the way God wants us to be, and try as we might we can't fix it. We are adept at many things and have many God given talents but this one we do not have.

Because of this broken image of God which we now have, we should find a way and indeed may want to find a way to restore the image, but we can't.

Wesley believed God's grace is given to every person and this particular grace he called prevenient grace, or preventing grace. He describes it this way:

> Salvation begins with what is usually termed (and very properly) *preventing grace*; including the first wish to please God, the first dawn of light concerning his will, and the first slight transient conviction of having sinned against him. All these imply some tendency toward life; some degree of salvation; the beginning of a deliverance from a blind, unfeeling heart, quite insensible of God and the things of God.[18]

Prevenient grace is God's gift of love to everyone; they just have to be willing to accept it. God gives us the power to accept his grace or reject his grace. By accepting his prevenient grace we have begun the way to salvation which is littered by God's many graces. Preventing here means just the opposite of what we today mean by it.

Preventing or prevenient grace is given to everybody, and when we say everybody we mean all of humanity, and this free gift allows everyone to choose for God or reject him.

Some have mistakenly assumed sex was the sin which separates us from God as if somehow sex was inherently bad, but this is just not true. Sex is God's gift to us but like everything else in life it can be

---

[18] Wesley, *Works*, 6:509

misused and abused. This is more like a story or talk given to us by our parents or someone who mistakenly believed the only way to keep us from having sex before marriage or before we should have it is to scare us by telling us how bad and evil a thing it is, complete with all of the bad things which can really happen to us if we don't heed their instruction. As a gift from God it is good, it is only we humans who can misuse God's good gift. It is pride, self-will, and unbelief which is sin, not sex. Much more about this is in our "Marriage with God" class which we will have later in the year.

Nobody could say it any better than it was said in one of the Wesley's hymns:

> Sinners, turn, why will ye die?
> God, your Maker, asks you why:
> God, who did your being give,
> Made you himself to live;
> He the total cause demands,
> Asks the work of his own hands,
> Why, ye thankless creatures, why
> Will ye cross his love, and die?
>
> Sinners, turn, why will ye die?
> God, your Saviour, asks you why:
> God, who did your souls retrieve,
> Died himself, that ye might live.
> Will you let him die in vain?
> Why, ye ransom'd sinners, why
> Crucify your Lord again?
> Will, you slight his grace, and die?
>
> Sinners, turn, why will ye die?
> God the Spirit, asks you why:
> He who all your lives hath strove,
> Woo'd you to embrace his love:
> Will you not his grace receive?
> Will you still refuse to live?
> Why, ye long-sought sinners, why
> Will you grieve your God, and die?
>
> Dead already? Dead within,
> Spiritually dead in sin:

Dead to God, while here you breathe,
Pant ye after second death?
Will you still in sin remain,
Greedy of eternal pain?
O ye dying sinners, why,
Why will you for ever die?[19]

"So you mean God's prevenient grace is given to Buddhists, followers of Islam as well as those who profess no religion" questioned Diane? "If this is the concept it is an amazing example of God's love for me."

"That's right," answered Todd, "God's prevenient grace is not just for those who are going to be or are trying to be Christian, and it's for everybody. That's what the book I read said also."

"That is nothing short of amazing," said Felista. "It's hard to believe God can love everyone that much. There are some I wouldn't think of giving it to if it was left up to me."

"And when we accept God's love it is really not our work but accepting what God has already done for us," said Barb. "That is wonderful news."

"So the Christian life is a life of grace," said Shawn, and the others agreed.

Article VIII—Of Free Will

The condition of man after the fall of Adam is such that he cannot turn and prepare himself, by his own natural strength and works, to faith, and calling upon God; wherefore we have no power to do good works, pleasant and acceptable to God, without the grace of God by Christ preventing us, that we may have a good will, and working with us, when we have that good will.[20]

The free will described here is not what we often think of, such as the free will to decide whether we will eat an apple or an orange, or go to the store before or after lunch, or read a book or watch TV. The free will we are talking about is so much more significant and important.

God has given us many gifts and he sends the rain on the just and the unjust, but this one gift is the gift allowing or giving us the

---

[19] Wesley, *Wesley's Hymns*, no. 6, vs. 1-4
[20] *The Book of Discipline of the United Methodist Church*, 65, 2012

power to choose him and a relationship with him. We call the gift of this power or grace, prevenient grace, and everyone has been given this grace. Some do not accept this grace and turn it down for a variety of other gods, but those who accept this gift and choose for him are on their way towards salvation, or the restoral of the image in which God created us.

This concept of prevenient grace rules out the competing concept which is from the foundation of the world God decided who would be saved and who would be damned. This is a Christian concept Wesley fought in his day, double predestination. Double predestination is the idea that we have no input in the decision of whether or not we can be saved, because God made this decision from before the world was created and there is nothing we can do about it.

Wesley presented the counter Christian concept of prevenient grace, which is the idea we can choose for God but we are able to make this choice only because God has given us the power and ability to do so. Wesley says the double predestination concept makes us like a machine or a rock which cannot do anything but follow the will of God or the will of the Devil and therefore we have no contribution or choice in the matter.

It naturally follows if everyone has been given the ability to choose for or against God we are therefore responsible for our choice and the repercussions of our choice. So, it is by God's grace we are given the power to choose but because of His grace and the power given to us, we are therefore responsible for our choice.

It also follows if prevenient grace is given to us so we have the power or ability to choose for or against God, and we choose for God, our life can be grace filled.

By accepting God we can now show works of contrition for our misused life. We can know all good gifts of the Christian life are not something we have earned by our good works. God is the author of them, he allows us the choice and it is our responsibility to make the choice for him, and grow in our relationship with him.

No one can explain it better than Wesley.

> The grace of love or God,
> whence cometh our salvation, is FREE
> IN ALL, and FREE FOR ALL.
>
> First, It is free IN ALL to whom
> it is given. It does not depend on any

> power or merit in man; no, not in any degree, neither in whole, nor in part. It does not in anywise depend either on the good works or righteousness of the receiver; not on anything he has done, or anything he is. It does not depend on his endeavours. It does not depend on his good tempers, or good desires, or good purposes and intentions; for all these flow from the free grace of God; they are the streams only, not the fountain. They are the fruits of free grace, and not the root. They are not the cause but the effects of it. Whatsoever good is in man, or is done by man, God is the author and doer of it. Thus is his grace free in all; that is, no way depending on any power or merit in man, but on God alone, who freely gave us his own Son, and "with him freely giveth us all things."[21]

This means that no matter how awful a sinner you are:
God loves you and wants you to accept his love and forgiveness.

If you are a thief—God loves you and wants you to accept his love and forgiveness.

If you are a liar—God loves you and wants you to accept his love and forgiveness.

If you are a cheat—God loves you and wants you to accept his love and forgiveness.

If you are adulterer—God loves you and wants you to accept his love and forgiveness.

If you are a gossip—God loves you and wants you to accept his love and forgiveness.

If you have followed other gods or tried to follow no god at all—God loves you and wants you to accept his love and forgiveness.

---

[21] Wesley, *Works*, 7:373-4

If you have hurt or murdered—God loves you and wants you to accept his love and forgiveness.

If you are addicted to drugs, alcohol or pornography or any other—God loves you and wants you to accept his love and forgiveness.

God wants you, and there is nothing you can do to remove yourself from his love. He will forgive and accept you back as one of his own if only, if only you will accept his love and not turn your back on him and his love.

"I'm going to read most of Psalm 139 to you because it speaks of God searching us in his love," said Pastor Bill.

O Lord, you have searched me and known me.
You know when I sit down and when I rise up:
    you discern my thoughts from far away.
You search out my path and my lying down,
    and are acquainted with all my ways.
Even before a word is on my tongue,
    O Lord, you know it completely.
You hem me in, behind and before,
    and lay your hand upon me.
Such knowledge is too wonderful for me'
    it is so high that I cannot attain it.

Where can I go from your spirit?
    Or where can I flee from your presence?
If I ascend to heaven, you are there;
    if I make my bed in Sheol, you are there.
If I take the wings of the morning
    and settle at the farthest limits of the sea,
even there your hand shall lead me,
    and your right hand shall hold me fast.
If I say, "Surely the darkness shall cover me
    and the light around me become night,"
even the darkness is not dark to you;
    the night is as bright as the day for darkness is as light to you.

For it was you who formed my inward parts;
    you knit me together in my mother's womb.
I praise you, for I am fearfully and wonderfully made.

    Wonderful are your works;
that I know very well.
    My frame was not hidden from you,
when I was being made in secret,
    intricately woven in the depths of the earth.
Your eyes beheld my unformed substance.
In your book were written
    all the days that were formed for me,
    when none of them as yet existed.
How weighty to me are your thoughts, O God!
    How vast is the sum of them!
I try to count them—they are more than the sand;
    I come to the end—I am still with you. Ps. 139 1-18

Todd said, "That is a powerful Scripture."

"Goodness," said Melinda. "It is amazing to me God is able to offer salvation to us but at the same time He allows us to make the decision for ourselves. I had heard as a child that God had already determined who was going to be saved and who wasn't. I certainly like this explanation a lot better than that one."

Shawn said "What impressed me is the fact we have a choice, we have the ability to choose but our choices for him does not make us good, we are only accepting the gift he already wants to give us. So really it is God always who saves and we can do nothing to make ourselves saved except to accept God's gift.

Felista said, "I haven't heard this expressed before but it makes me happy to hear it presented this way because I did not understand before exactly how these things worked."

Diane agreed with Felista's comment and understanding.

"I was interested in the concept of free will," said Barb. "I heard about free will when I was in our church's youth group but did not understand it. They weren't able to make it as clear for me as this has been. Maybe I was just a little too young to fully understand."

"I'm all for that free will," happily stated Felista. I think it is the greatest gift from God. It's wonderful."

James replied "Felista's all for free will of any kind."

Todd said, "This area is much like the book I have talked about. The book and Pastor Bill are in firm agreement."

SCRIPTURE

The Lord God said to the serpent,
"Because you have done this,
  cursed are you among all animals,
  and among all wild creatures;
upon your belly you shall go,
  and dust you shall eat
  all the days of your life.
I will put enmity between you and the woman,
  and between your offspring and hers;
he will strike your head
  and you will strike his heel."
To the woman he said,
  "I will greatly increase your pangs in childbearing;
  in pain you shall bring forth children,
yet your desire will be for your husband,
  and he shall rule over you."
And to the man he said,
  "Because you have listened to the voice of your wife,
  and have eaten of the tree
about which I commanded you,
  'You shall not eat of it,'
cursed is the ground because of you;
  in toil you shall eat of it all the days of your life;
thorns and thistles it shall bring forth for you;
  and you shall eat the plants of the field.
By the sweat of your face
  you shall eat bread
until you return to the ground,
  for out of it you were taken;
you are dust,
  and to dust you shall return.'"
    (Genesis 3:14-19)

PRAYER

Most gracious heavenly Father, though we have not deserved your mercy and love you loved us enough to send your Son to the earth to live, preach and yes, even to die upon a cross for us so that we might be able to return to the fellowship with you for which we were created, we give you thanks for your great mercy.

Bless us as we study together to learn of your mighty works on our behalf. Come into our lives more fully and may we be aware of your presence in things both within and without.

Bless this group as we learn together, share together, and fellowship together as a group of those who are your church in this world.

In the name of Christ we ask these things. Amen

CHAPTER 5. QUESTIONS

1. Are we able to become better and better as a person and as a society or do we stand in the need for help from God? Why do you think so?

2. Was God somehow the source of humanity's separation from God? Did he make sure the serpent fooled Eve and Adam followed Eve's advice? If not God, who was responsible for the so called fall of humanity?

3. People can do many things. We have made lots of progress in many fields, why do we need God if we are able to do all of these wonderful things?

4. What is preventing or prevenient grace? Why is it so important in our understanding of the relationship between God and humanity?

5. If prevenient grace is the gift of God to us, why is there still sin?

6. In what way has God given us the ability to choose between himself and any other god?

7. What does Wesley mean by Free In All, and Free For All?

CHAPTER 6 Methodist Beliefs (cont.)

Article V—Of the Sufficiency of the Holy Scriptures for Salvation

The Holy Scripture containeth all things necessary to salvation; so that whatsoever is not read therein, nor may be proved thereby, is not to be required of any man that it should be believed as an article of faith, or be thought requisite or necessary to salvation. In the name of the Holy Scripture we do understand those canonical books of the Old and New Testament of whose authority was never any doubt in the church.

All of the books of the New Testament, as they are commonly received, we do receive and account canonical.[22]

Article VI—Of the Old Testament

The Old Testament is not contrary to the New; for both in the Old and New Testament everlasting life is offered to mankind by Christ; who is the only Mediator between God and man, being both God and Man. Wherefore they are not to be heard who feign that the old fathers did look only for transitory promises. Although the law given from God by Moses as touching ceremonies and rites doth not bind Christians, nor ought the civil precepts thereof of necessity be received in any commonwealth; yet notwithstanding, no Christian whatsoever is free from the obedience of the commandments which are called moral.[23]

The class gathered again for coffee and refreshments. It was a nice day so far, hardly a cloud in the sky but the promise for rain in the next day or two.

Jim began, "Finally, I'm happy to be discussing something I know a little about. The Bible is not quite an unknown quantity to me because I read a lot of it while in the youth group of my church. In fact, I had to read the Scripture lesson in the church at times."

"I too was more familiar with this area than the others we have studied so far," said Diane. "I have a Student Bible and use that when I have questions and I certainly have a lot of them so I read until I get tired tracking down the information."

---

[22] *The Book of Discipline of the United Methodist Church*, 64-5, 2012
[23] Ibid, 65

Shawn responded, "I was raised on the King James Version and even had one given to me by my parents a long time ago, but they later gave me a student Bible of the RSV."

"I was given my family Bible and it has the dates of births and marriages in it," said Melinda. "I really need to bring it up to date though, by adding Todd and my marriage and the births of our two sons."

Felista said, 'I've started reading "The Message" and I really enjoy it. He really brings the message home to me.

Todd asked Pastor Bill, "Does it make any difference what version of the bible one reads?"

Pastor Bill said, "The question Todd asks is an excellent one and we will see if we can't answer some of it now."

Probably the two most common versions, those prepared by committees of various denominations, are the New Revised Standard Version (NRSV), and the New International Version (NIV), but some like the American Standard Version (ASV) upon which the Revised Standard Versions are based. However, for those who prefer the beauty of the language, many prefer the King James Version (KJV), or New King James Version (NKJV). One translation by a single author that has a lot of acceptance today is The Message by Eugene Peterson. Pastor Bill went on to say that when he read the Bible for himself or always from the pulpit, he would read the NRSV, NIV and The Message and select the one he liked best, the one which best presented the point he was trying to make and was clearest for the congregation to understand.

Diane said, "I've read some from another version and it seemed to be like the NIV which I usually read."

"When I was in the church years ago they used the King James Version but I'm now also reading the NRSV and I like it," said Melinda.

"This information was very helpful," said Todd.

Pastor Bill then said "normally the Study Bibles of any of these Bibles have a lot of extra information in them, both in the front and the back which give history of the versions of the Bible and a lot of additional information."

Pastor bill showed his Bible to the class. It was the NRSV, which was the New Oxford Annotated Bible. In the front of the Bible it told how to use it profitably. It also had an introduction to each book in the Bible. In the back of the book was an abundance of articles and information such as "Modern Approaches to Biblical Study," "Characteristics of Hebrew Poetry"; "Literary Forms in the Gospels": "English Versions of the Bible": "Survey of Geography, History, Archaeology" and "Weights and Measures." Some of the Bibles even have the apocrypha which are the books written between Our Old Testament and New Testament and are not accepted by Protestants.

Shawn looked at Diane and said to Pastor Bill "I always wanted to know how to read the Bible. I've read some here and there but I can't seem to get the hang of it."

Melinda spoke up and said "I thought it was like any other book so I started at the front, at Genesis, but I got bogged down soon. I got lost in a lot of begets and other things which weren't interesting to me."

Pastor Bill told the group, "We have and will be making great statements about the Bible and what is contained in the Bible."

The Bible is unlike any other book you will read. To begin with it was written over a great many years and by a great many people. Also, unlike copyrighted material we are familiar with today they thought nothing about making clarifying statements in the Scriptures at a later date. Also some of the books are given the name of a well known person but that particular person did not write it. They used the person's name because they were well known or were written in an effort to communicate what the person taught or thought.

The Hebrew text was originally written with no vowels. Many years later the vowels were added in. For instance in the Old Testament the name for God in many translations is Yahweh, but the original would have been YHWH.

Also the original did not have periods or commas which were added when the vowels were included. Think of this group of letters, "heisnowhere." Does this say he is "no where" or he is "now here?" We have to thank those who inserted these additions to the original text because they have helped us considerably in understanding them.

I would suggest you start with the Gospel of John. Of all the Gospels it tells about Jesus and what he means to us in a way none of the others do. After you have read it a few times you can read the other Gospels.

Also you may want to read the Psalms in a month and then repeat. It is simple, there are 150 Psalms and 30 days so you divine 150 by 30 and you have only 5 Psalms to read each day. An interesting way to read them is like this 1, 31, 61, 91, and 121 on the first day and then the next day read 2, 32, 62, 92, and 122 and so on until you have finished the Psalms.

Questioning how to read the Bible is a common one asked by many people. As short of extra time as we are we need all the help we can get. There are programs on the internet which show you how to read the Bible in a year, but I wouldn't try such an aggressive program until you have read a few of the books a few times and gotten familiar with them.

Both Shawn and Melinda expressed their appreciation for the help Pastor Bill had given them and they would try both the Gospel of John and the Psalms. Others in the group nodded their agreement also.

When we look at the Bible we know the books in our Bible are the same pretty much throughout Protestantism. As we discussed earlier, the Catholic Churches have a different number from Protestants and they differ from each other. They have more books in their Bible than we do. However, we all believe in the Bible and the bulk of it is the same for all of us.

The faith of we Protestants is founded on the Bible and if this foundation is allowed to shift to anything else, Protestantism, like a pricked balloon, looses its steam and real, vital Christianity suffers and goes down.

We look to the Bible to find what God wants for our lives. Many books are written and sold, they come in today and are gone tomorrow, but the Bible has endured. The real things, the permanent things of God continue long after the 10 Best lists are gone and are forgotten. The Bible was around long before those lists and will continue long after they cease.

We discussed the many Old Testament characters we have heard about and we also like to read about Jesus and what he said, and taught, and did. We like to read about Paul and the many others who were the followers of Jesus.

The Bible is as relevant today as it has always been. Though times change, cultures change, and ideas change, the message of God is the same. Sometimes we have to figure out how to present it to a new culture or time but the message is eternally the same.

The Bible tells us everything we need to know about God. We read and know God is the creator of the entire universe. Everything we see, everything we feel, everything, has come from the hand of a creator God. He alone is God, there is no other. He is Lord over all. We are still searching to learn about his creation.

We also learn about humanity. Rather than read the newspaper to hear about humanity and our good/bad deeds, the Scriptures insist we do not really know who we are until we understand how to look at ourselves through the perspective we see in the Scriptures.

We find humanity is created, we have been created by God and He has created us to be dependent on Him because we are his creation. We are mortal, but God is immortal.

As we discussed earlier, we are special because of all living things we are created different. We were created in the image of God. God has created us for himself.

We also know we are sinners; we have destroyed the image in which we were created. We learn all of us have competing loyalties or desires and we often choose the wrong ones. God has given us the power to accept him and reject all of them but it is truly a fight.

The Bible tells us all we need to know about humanity and God getting together in a relationship of love. Not wishy-washy stuff which is not love, but love which wants tremendously the best for the other. Because God has first loved us we are able to respond to His love with our own love. God has not forced us to love him because love cannot be forced. Love can only be accepted, love can only be shown by two who are bound to each other, real love gives to the other and then the gift has to be accepted and a loving response can be given.

The Scriptures are God's word to us. Though we do not believe God wrote the actual words, he certainly inspired the writers who did write the words. The message is there of God's dealings with human beings, our response, and God's love in sending a Son to perform the mighty work of the possibility of salvation for the whole world.

We have our Bible and we are not going to add anything else to it, neither are we going to take anything away from it. We try not to read the Bible with a cookie-cutter mentality of accepting what we want or what agrees with us and rejecting those parts we don't like. We are to come to the Scriptures with open minds and hearts to find what God is saying to us. We are human, so we can't actually do away with our prejudices etc… but the more open we can be to receive, the better.

The Holy Spirit was certainly guiding these authors in their prayerful thoughts and understanding about God, humanity, and the relationship which should exist and the relationship which does exist between God and us and between us and our fellow beings. Because we are all sinners the relationship which should exist between us does not always exist.

The wonderful news for us is we do not have to look elsewhere, in other books or areas, to find the way of salvation. Everything necessary for us to know is found in this one book. Naturally, we can and should read other books to understand what we cannot understand in the Bible by our own reading but the Bible still remains basic.

The books of the Old Testament are Scriptures for us as well as those of the New Testament. These are the Scriptures read, commented upon, and used by Jesus. He used them and understood them to be Scriptures and nowhere did he tell us to dismiss them.

As far as I know there was never any doubt for Christians about the Old Testament being scripture. They tell us of God's dealings with the Jews and all people. They tell us of the desire and search for the Messiah. They tell us some of what the Messiah will accomplish. They point toward the one who would come.

These are the wonderful words of God's people, about God and his dealings with them. Jesus had the same Father who found the Jews in the Old Testament. We Christians need to read the Old Testament in light of the New Testament and the revealing of God in Christ we find there.

John Wesley used a method which we today call the Quadrilateral Method for understanding Scriptures which are difficult or perplexing to us. Though he did not call it that and did not put it down exactly this way we can glean a lot from it. The term was given to us by Albert Outler, Methodist and Wesleyan scholar, and if John became familiar with it he undoubtedly would have put scripture as the most important of the four. The others must always bow to the preeminence of scripture.

The first tool we are to use is Christian tradition. By this Wesley means primarily the first century Fathers and the rich tradition of the Anglican Church. We Methodists today really have a much expanded view of tradition and therefore we consider the consensus of the faithful which not only includes the Early Fathers and the Anglican Church but the whole church from Biblical times until now. Methodists are open to learning from the tradition of the Roman Catholics, Lutherans, and Presbyterians etc… We should do well, however, to once more study carefully the early Church Fathers because we have lost much of their teachings by being too caught up in our day, its experiences, and the current pop psychology. Where scripture is silent we can listen to tradition, especially the tradition of the early church for guidance.

The second tool we should use is other Scriptures on the same topic. One who reads much of Wesley will find himself constantly reading quotes from Scripture. No other book by any author I have read quotes as much Scripture in their sermons and tracts. His work is rich with passages from them. Wesley says he was a person of one book and this book is the scriptures. He read extensively but the Bible was the final authority for his preaching and his thought. Scripture is often found in his writings as Wesley's thought and wrote. He used Scripture often as quotations found apart from his thought, but mainly they were used as expressions of his thought.

The third tool is reason. Reason is important because God has given it to us and if you exclude reason you cannot interpret the Scriptures, Christian tradition or experience. Reason has its limits but it is important and should be in the arsenal of the Christian. It is also true and important for us to remember Wesley said religion is a matter of the heart and not a matter of correct beliefs. This thought needs to temper our use of reason.

The fourth tool is experience and by experience Wesley means our experience with God and our fellow humans. The experience Wesley is interested in is the experience which comes from reading the Scriptures. To Wesley it is important to have his and others experience be consistent with what he reads and understands from the scriptures. The Christian experiences which we have should be found in the Scriptures. If the type of experience we are discussing as Christian and is not found in the Scriptures we should be a little leery of calling such experience Christian.

This is just a short sketch of what Wesley thought of and passed on to his followers about how to read and interpret the Scriptures accurately. To quote him:

> I want to know one thing,—the way to heaven; how to land safe on that happy shore. God himself has condescended to teach the way: For this very end he came from heaven. He hath written it down in a book. O give me that book! At any price give me the book of God! I have it; Here is

knowledge enough for me. Let me be *homo unis libri*. Here then I am, far from the busy ways of men. I sit down alone: Only God is here. In his presence I open, I read his book; for this end, to find the way to heaven. Is there a doubt concerning the meaning of what I read? Does anything appear dark or intricate? I lift up my heart to the Father of Lights:—"Lord, is it not thy word, 'If any man lack wisdom, let him ask of God?' Thou 'givest liberally, and upbraidest not.' Thou hast said, 'If any be willing to do thy will, he shall know.' I am willing to do, let me know, thy will.' I then search after and consider parallel passages of Scripture, "comparing spiritual with things spiritual." I meditate thereon with all the attention and earnestness of which my mind is capable. If any doubt still remains, I consult those who are experienced in the things of God; and then the writings whereby, being dead, they yet speak. And what I thus learn, that I teach."[24]

---

[24] Wesley, *Works*, 5:3-4

SCRIPTURE

Then God said, "Let us make humankind in our image, according to our likeness: and let them have dominion over the fish of the sea, and over the birds of the air, and over the cattle, and over all the wild animals of the earth, and over every creeping thing that creeps upon the earth."

So God created humankind in his image
in the image of God he created them;
male and female he created them.

God saw everything that he had made, and indeed, it was very good. And there was evening and there was morning, the sixth day. (Genesis 1:26-27, 31)

PRAYER

Our Heavenly Father, You have been incredibly creative and loving in your dealings with us. You have also been consistent in your love whereas we have waffled and drifted and been inconsistent.

We give you thanks for your great mercy and your providing us with a holy book, the Bible in which we find all that is necessary for our salvation. Help us to read and understand the message you are giving us so we might find, accept, and travel the paths you would have us go.

Bless our studies together as we share with each other what we have found of your message to us we ask in the name of Jesus our Christ. Amen.

CHAPTER 6. QUESTIONS

1. What are the two or three most common and used versions of the Bible? Which ones do you like best? Why?

2. What are some of the resources for reading and understanding the Bible which are found in some of the Student Bibles?

3. Are we today really different from humans in the times of the Old and New Testaments? Why?

4. Why are the books of the Old Testament relevant today? After all they were written before Christ was born.

5. What tools for reading and understanding Scripture are given to us through what is called Wesley's Quadrilateral?

CHAPTER 7 Methodist Beliefs (cont.)

Article IX—Of the Justification of Man

We are accounted righteous before God only for the merit of our Lord and Saviour Jesus Christ, by faith, and not for our own works or deservings. Wherefore, that we are justified by faith, only, is a most wholesome doctrine, and very full of comfort.[25]

Article XII—Of Sin After Justification

Not every sin willingly committed after justification is the sin against the Holy Ghost, and unpardonable. Wherefore, the grant of repentance is not to be denied to such as fall into sin after justification. After we have received the Holy Ghost, we may depart from grace given, and fall into sin, and, by the grace of God, rise again and amend our lives. And therefore they are to be condemned who say they can no more sin as long as they live here; or deny the place of forgiveness to such as truly repent.[26]

Sanctification—Though not an Article, it was accepted by the church in 1939 and is an important Methodist doctrine.

Sanctification is that renewal of our fallen nature by the Holy Ghost, received through faith in Jesus Christ, whose blood of atonement cleanseth from all sin; whereby we are not only delivered from the guilt of sin, but are washed from its pollution, saved from its power, and are enabled, through grace, to love God with all our hearts and to walk in his holy commandments blameless.[27]

As they were gathering together, sipping their coffee and discussing their kids, they were still laughing at something Glenda said to the group. A few days earlier Barb was out of the house and Jim was watching Glenda and trying to get some work done. Glenda in her interested and curious manner was peppering him with questions. Finally in exasperation, Jim told her that sometimes she reminded him of somebody with constipation of the brain and diarrhea of the mouth. Immediately, knowing he had said something wrong, he stopped, hoping that Glenda would forget it, and she did until the day of the get together when somebody asked her how she was and she told them her

---

[25] *The Discipline of the United Methodist Church*, 65, 2012
[26] Ibid, 66
[27] Ibid, 70

daddy said she had constipation of the brain and diarrhea of the mouth, and a good laugh was had again by all.

Diane said, "I really found this chapter to be clarifying for me. I had heard the two words justification and sanctification bandied around but really did not understand them or the difference between them."

Shawn spoke up, "It was a difficult area for me and I certainly hope I will receive some additional insights from this session.

James agreed, "I really enjoyed reading about the Methodist beliefs."

"You would," said Felista.

Barb said, "I really enjoyed this area because it reminded me of my church in high school and what I learned there."

Jim laughingly said, "Here all this time I thought the main thing you learned there was about me," and the others laughed.

Barb replied, "I knew all I needed to know about you in five minutes," and they all laughed again.

"Whooee," said Felista, "you can scope out a man in five minutes but this section takes a little longer."

Pastor Bill said they would consider these three articles together because they kind of fit together and make sense when they are joined together in the discussion.

If you are a Christian or if you see others going awry or even if you only think about what happens when we depart this life, justification by faith becomes an important concept for us to consider and ponder.

Some say when we die nothing more happens, it is just the end. The body decays, memories of the departed fade, and finally end altogether. This is certainly a pessimistic view and one I do not believe, but there are those who think this way or at least they say they do. If this position is true then why not make the seven deadly sins your bright stars of life and get all of everything you can, as much as you can, because when you are gone you certainly can't get any more? I guess some people really believe this way.

Jesus tells us there is a different way of thinking and a different way of living. Jesus did not put his ideas in a book of theology for us; he lived his life and preached to those who heard. His followers have prayed, thought, read, and written about how to understand these things.

We Protestants talk about justification by faith because this concept is the foundation of all our hope because while we are at war with God, separated from him, with our broken image of God we cannot participate in the peace and joy which only he can give.

In order to fully understand this doctrine of justification by faith we need to tread on some other theological toes by backing up and really set the scene for our better understanding of the process.

We are created holy as God is holy; merciful as he is merciful; and perfect in love as God is perfect in love. And as God is love so we can love. We are likewise made for an eternity with God. We are pure as God is pure and know not sin or evil.

Because we were created in God's image we were given a law which required perfect obedience. Created with the love of God in our hearts we were given the commandment not to eat of the fruit of one tree in the garden because if we did eat of the fruit we would die. What a wonderful time Adam had with God and his helpmate when everything was right in God's love!

But, as we know, Adam and Eve did disobey God and did what they were commanded not to do. Because of this rebellious action on Adam's part Adam was condemned by the righteousness of God. Adam's sentence, which was promised, was given. Adam's soul died because it was separated from God. Adam's became corruptible and we would now die a physical death. Because Adam was now dead in spirit, dead to God, and dead in sin, he was well on his way to death eternal; the destruction of both body and soul.

Through one person sin and death entered the world and it has been there ever since. This has been our condition throughout time until God, loving the world so much, when the time was right he sent his Son into the world, and the Son tasted death for everyone and God reconciled the world to himself.

Terry Bell in his "The Love Ethic," tells us of God's love.

> Agape (Love) [parenthesis mine]...extends itself for no other reason than extending itself. It is a going out to rather than a receiving. It is unexplainable in human terms for it is uncaused by our worth. God does not love us because we are worthy. We are worthy because he loves us. Agape is indifferent to human merit. Such

> parables in the Gospels as the Prodigal Son, the Vineyard, the Sower, the Lost Sheep and the Unmerciful Servant bring out this aspect that Agape is fully the initiative of God.
>
> In the Christian faith, Agape not only comes from God, it is God (that is, it is the very essence of God). No other world religion can identify with the teaching that God is Love in this same sense. Love is not just an act or an attitude of God. It is the very essence of God.[28]

Now, for the sake of his Son, for what he did and suffered for us there is one way, a way he himself graciously allows us to accept and thereby our sins and the punishment for them have been forgiven and we are reinstated in a relationship with him and our souls which were dead have been restored to the spiritual life, even life eternal.

This is the background of the doctrine of justification by faith and helps in understanding the reasons for it and how it is applied.

A. Justification

Now let's discuss what justification is and clarify the differences between justification and sanctification. Justification is what God does for us through the work of his Son. Sanctification is what God works in us by his Spirit. This sounds like an easy distinction, yet it is difficult and will be made clearer in a few minutes.

"I'm so glad you clarified it for us," commented Shawn. The others laughed at Shawn's humor.

One common mistaken idea about justification is the idea God is deceived or fooled somehow and he thinks we are without sin when we really are sinful beings. God is not fooled; he knows our situation and his judgment of us is justified because it is the truth.

The truth of the matter is justification means our past sins are forgiven. It is God's act for the sake and work of the Son which gives

---

[28] Bell, Terry, *The Love Ethic*, 84

remission or forgiveness of our sins. All of our sins are forgiven. All our past sins of thought, word, or deed are covered and are not held against us. Justification does not go forward, magically clearing out and forgiving all future sins no matter what we may do in the future.

Then we must ask ourselves, who does God justify and forgive of their sins? God justifies the ungodly, the ungodly of every kind. Those who are righteous or who believe they are righteous and therefore do not think they need and therefore do not seek forgiveness do not receive forgiveness. Only sinners can be forgiven their sins. Forgiveness is forgiveness of sin. Without sin there is no need for forgiveness, is there?

Some people think we must make ourselves holy before we can be justified. This is a misconception because we can't do it ourselves, anyway. It is God who justifies the sinner. The sinner, not the one who thinks he's all right, is justified.

This love of God's goes out to all kinds of sinners and seeks them all to accept the love and grace of justification. As the Scriptures say, those who are sick and in need of a physician are those who go to and will receive a physician. God's love for us comes to us long before we are justified.

As Wesley said:

> If we take this in its utmost extent, it will include all that is wrought in the soul by what is frequently termed 'natural conscience,' but more properly, 'preventing grace'; all the drawings of the Father—the desires after God which if we yield to them, increase more and more: all that light wherewith the Son of God 'enlighteneth every one that cometh into the world'—showing every man 'to do justly, to love mercy, and to walk humbly with his God'; all the convictions which His Spirit, from time to time, works in every child of man—although it is true, the generality of men stifle them as soon as possible, and after a while forget, or at least deny, that they ever had them at all.[29]

There is only one thing which allows for justification or is needed to be justified, and that is faith in God. There are many different ways of understanding this faith. The main emphasis of this faith is a conviction God was in Christ reconciling the world to him and our having a sure trust and confidence Christ died for my sins, he loves me and gave himself for me. Whenever a person has this faith, this confidence, God justifies him.

We may and probably will feel repentance before being justified but this repentance does not justify. It does show us we are not good enough for him, and we can bring nothing to him. After we believe in him any works done are done through faith.

Faith is the necessity and the only thing necessary for justification. Justification does not and will not occur without faith—faith alone is required. So long as we do not have this faith we will not and cannot be justified.

This seems too simple but it is true. This faith is a sure trust and reliance that God has and will forgive our sins and he has accepted us into his favor. All of this happens from God's side because of the work of his Son. It does not happen because we have or can do anything to bring or force it to come about.

God knows we are sinners but just as he made Christ to be sin for us, because he treated him as a sinner, and punished him for our sins, so he treats us as if we were righteous when we believe in him. He does not then punish us for our sins; rather he treats us as though we were guiltless and righteous.

Faith is the necessity and the only necessity for one to be justified. In this way it is by the grace of God we are saved and not through any work, thought, idea, or deed of our own. All is of grace, all is a gift, we just have to accept God's gift by trusting and believing in him. Justification is God's work not ours.

---

[29] Wesley, *Standard Sermons*, 2, 445

Wesley put it this way:

> *Thus look unto Jesus!* There is *the Lamb of God*, who *taketh away thy sins!* Plead thou no works, no righteousness of thine own! no humility, contrition, sincerity! In nowise. That were, in very deed, to deny the Lord that bought thee. No: plead thou, singly, the blood of the covenant, the ransom paid for thy proud, stubborn, sinful soul. Who art thou, that now seest and feelest both thine inward and outward ungodliness? Thou art the man! I want thee for my Lord! I challenge *thee* for a child of God by faith! The Lord hath need of thee. Thou who feelest thou art just fit for hell, art just fit to advance his glory; the glory of his free grace, justifying the ungodly and him that worketh not. O come quickly! Believe in the Lord Jesus; and thou, even thou, art reconciled to God.[30]

B. Sin After Justification

Wesley and we Methodists believe after being justified we may sin but fortunately we can be forgiven our sins and be restored by the grace of God to the saving relationship with him.

"Wouldn't it be awful," said Pastor Bill, "if we had to be perfect from there on after we were first justified? If this were the case we might as well give it up now. Even though we sin after being justified we can be restored to the relationship with God through the mighty works God performed through his Son Jesus."

"I certainly could not do it," said Barb. "I have trouble trying to hold my temper with one child. Wonder what it will be like with two?"

"Don't think it would be possible for me either," said Shawn. "Sometimes they just seem to be trying to make things difficult."

---

[30] Wesley, *Works*, 5:64

Melinda said, "It makes me so happy that I don't have to do all this work myself, because I know I can't."

"That's so true girl, it's just not possible," said Felista.

James Brown mumbled, "That's what I have been saying, Felista."

Through quoting Scripture Wesley says those who are holy or righteous in God's judgment may finally fall from grace. Also, one who has enough faith to have a clear conscience may finally fall. Again, those who have been grafted into the good olive tree, which is the spiritual, invisible church, may likewise fall. Again, those who are branches of Christ, the true vine, may fall from grace. Even those who know Christ and have escaped the pollutions of the world, may yet fall. Those who see the light of the glory of God in the face of Jesus Christ and who have received the Holy Spirit may also fall. Those who live by faith may fall and even those who have been sanctified may likewise fall. Wesley gives Scriptures for all of these statements.

Wesley is saying no matter where you are in the Christian faith you can fall. He does not say you will fall and neither does he say you can't be restored. He is saying you can fall, not you must fall. He was here arguing against the doctrine of double predestination which was that from before the foundation of this world God determined who was going to be saved and who was going to be damned and there was nothing we could do which would change this selection. In other words, we could as well be a rock or robot because we had no choice or say in the matter—we are either God's or the Devil's without any reference or ability or an input from us.

John Wesley was sure even if one was justified they could fall away from God's free grace. If one is a true believer, or is holy or righteous in the judgment of God, they may fall from grace, and he gives Ezekiel 18:24 as his evidence.

Further, if a person who is endued with the faith so they have a good conscience, they may finally fall, and for that he quotes I Timothy 1:18, 19.

Again, even those who are grafted into the good olive tree, the spiritual, invisible Church, may finally fall. The Scripture for this is Romans 11: 17 and following.

Those who are branches of Christ, the true vine, may yet finally fall from grace. He points to John 15:1 and following as his basis for this assertion.

Those who know Christ, and by this knowledge have escaped the pollutions for the world, may yet fall back on those pollutions and perish everlastingly. The Scripture for this assertion is II Peter 2:20.

Those who see the light of the glory of God in the face of Jesus Christ, and who have been made partakers of the Holy Ghost, of the witness and the fruits of the Spirit, may also fall and perish. He quotes Hebrews 6:4-6 for this assertion.

Even those who live by faith may yet fall from God, and thereby perish. For this statement he quotes from Hebrews 10:38

Finally those who are sanctified by the blood of the covenant may also fall and perish everlastingly.

He quotes other Scripture to make his point such as Matthew 5:13, Matthew 12:43-45 and 24:10 following, Luke 21:34, John 8:31, 32 and many others.[31] Wesley concludes this area by saying:

> "Why, then you make salvation conditional." I make it neither conditional nor unconditional. But I declare just what I find in the Bible, neither more nor less; namely, that it is bought for every child of man, and actually given to every one that believeth. If you call this conditional salvation, God made it so from the beginning of the world; and hath declared it so to be, at sundry times and in divers manners; of old by Moses and the Prophets, and in later times by Christ and his Apostles

> Then I never can be saved; for I can perform no conditions; for I can do nothing." No, nor I, nor any man under heaven,—without the grace of God.[32]

---

[31] Wesley, *Works*, 10:252-4
[32] Ibid, 10:254

"Wow, that really makes salvation a dynamic process, doesn't it," exclaimed Todd. "You are justified by faith for your past sins but being human we will sin again so it's wonderful we can come back to God and ask for forgiveness and receive it."

"Yes," replied Felista, "You are living with God in a relationship, and that relationship is dynamic, just as the relationship with others is dynamic."

"I had never really considered it like that," said Shawn, "I just assumed once you were justified it was all over, but I really did not think much about it."

This we believe wrong (that humans have no choice and therefore are not responsible) because we believe God has given us the grace to accept him and we aren't robots, we have also been given the power to reject him. This power, this grace, God has given us for life, not just for once. We always have a choice of whether to choose God and his way for us and this choice is moment-by-moment. God never stops giving his grace; it is we who may not accept this grace.

Who among us believes we always know and do God's will? I don't but thankfully God is a loving God and even if we fall or stumble or sin, he is willing to forgive and restore us by his grace.

There is a dynamic here in Wesleyan thought. Like a relationship with any other person, there is change over time. We are closer at some times and more distant at others. We may even part company or end the relationship at any time. God has given us the same power of choice so we may choose him and a loving relationship with him or we may turn our backs on that relationship at any time.

C. Sanctification (Christian Perfection)

"As far as Christian Perfection is concerned, we have to be careful in our explanation of it so we don't mislead anybody," said Pastor Bill.

Jim said, "You mean we have to be perfect in everything, how in the world can that be? Even I know this to be impossible."

"Well Jim; you think you are always right," said Barb.

"I had a difficult time with the concept of Christian Perfection," said Melinda, "but I heard about it in church when I was a teenager."

Felista said, "I want to go on to Perfection, it sure sounds good to me."

"I think my wife is perfect just as she is." said Shawn.

Diane responded, "You're just trying to get on my good side Shawn, but I like it, you can just keep on talking."

Pastor Bill said, "We have to be careful in our explanation here. We are not made perfect physically or mentally. We may have any number of impediments in either. We may be misinformed, totally mistaken in our ideas. We may not be able to spell or do math or speak foreign languages, but these have nothing to do with Christian Perfection anyway."

"Thank goodness," said Shawn.

There are many descriptions of Christian Perfection and remember we are talking about no other kind of perfection except Christian. Wesleyans believe there are three ways Christian Perfection can be described or understood. The first is they have such a purity of intention they have dedicated all of life to God. The second description is they have the entire mind which was in Christ which enables us to walk as Christ walked and therefore we have the renewal of our hearts in the image of God. The third way of looking at Christian Perfection is to say they love God with all their heart and their neighbor as themselves.

You see the perfection sought and talked about is Christian Perfection, nothing more and certainly nothing less. It has nothing to do with any other type of perfection we may think about.

The process of Christian Perfection is begun when a person is justified. Normally God does not also grant Christian Perfection with justification because it is usually a process of growth in the Christian life culminating in Christian Perfection.

A Christian, after justification, begins a life of prayer, Scripture reading, attending to the sacraments, and in every way possible tries to learn the will of God for their lives and to live as God would have them live.

Though Christian Perfection is normally a process of growth, there is likewise a time before and a time after receiving the fullness of this gift from God because the only thing necessary to receive this grace is faith. Just as faith is necessary for justification it is also necessary for Christian Perfection. There is nothing we can do to earn this gift, it is given by the grace of God, but we are to seek after this gift in the hope of receiving it.

> A man may be dying for some time; yet he does not, properly speaking, die, till the instant the soul is separated from the body; and in that instant he lives the life of eternity. In like manner, he may be dying to sin for some time; yet he is not dead to sin till sin is separated from his soul; and in that instant he lives the full life of love. And as the change undergone, when the body dies, is of a different kind, and infinitely greater than any we had known before, yes, such as till then it is impossible to conceive; so the change wrought when the soul dies to sin, is of a different kind, and infinitely greater than any before, and than any can conceive till he experience it. Yet he still grows in grace, in the knowledge of Christ, in the love and image of God; and will do so, not only till death, but to all eternity.[33]

Though we believe most people do not receive this gift of Christian Perfection until shortly before death, we do not have to wait until then. We should seek it with the expectation this is a gift of God's grace and as such can be given at any time. There is no reason why we should resign ourselves to waiting when we can receive this gift earlier.

We do not speak often today about Christian Perfection. You don't hear many sermons about it or God's continual working in our hearts and lives, ever urging, ever pulling us towards Christian Perfection but we should be striving for and expectantly believing God will do what he has promised if we have faith he will fulfill his promises.

Undoubtedly some may think Christian Perfection is too close to the old idea of getting better day by day. This idea is the human being is capable of becoming a better and better person and also our

---

[33] Wesley, *Works*, 11, 402

society was capable of getting better and better each day. This growth was based on our development as human beings and with the strength and energy of human beings.

This is very different from Christian Perfection which is from God and a gift from God based on our faith in him and our working with him to grow in his love.

What! Never speak one evil word,
  Or rash, or idle, or unkind!
O how shall I, most gracious Lord,
  This mark of true perfection find?

Thy sinless mind in me reveal;
  Thy Spirit's platitude impart;
And all my spotless life shall tell
  The abundance of a loving heart.

Saviour, I long to testify
  The fullness of thy saving grace;
O might thy Spirit the blood apply,
  Which bought for me the sacred peace!

Forgive and make my nature whole;
  My inbred malady remove;
To perfect health restore my soul,
  To perfect holiness and love.[34]

"Wow, we did cover a lot today," said Shawn. "I was interested and didn't realize justification was for past sins and did not include future sins, but it does make sense that when God forgives us he forgives what we are and not what we are going to be or do."

"I was interested in Christian Perfection," said Barb. "We did talk about it when I was in high school and in church but I really did not understand it. I somehow got the idea it was a lot of work and if you did it just right you could receive Christian Perfection, something like earning a Girl Scout badge."

Todd said, "The book I have been reading and talking about, "Wesley's Wars" had a chapter on the topic of Christian Perfection and I got a lot out of it."

---

[34] Wesley, *Hymns*, #363

"I still want to be a Perfected Christian," said Felista. "I really would."

"Whatever Felista wants, Felista gets," James, her husband replied.

The others laughed at this interplay.

SCRIPTURE

For while we were still weak, at the right time Christ died for the ungodly. Indeed, rarely will anyone die for a righteous person—though perhaps for a good person someone might actually dare to die. But God proves his love for us in that while we still were sinners Christ died for us. Much more surely then, now that we have been justified by his blood, will we be saved through him from the wrath of God. For if while we were enemies, we were reconciled to God through the death of his Son, much more surely, having been reconciled, will we be saved by his life. But more than that, we even boast in God through our Lord Jesus Christ, through whom we have now received reconciliation. (Romans 5:6-11)

PRAYER

Our Father, what great things we learn about you. Your love for us, even though we did not know you, did not love you, did not claim you, is so great you sent your Son to come into our world to tell us about you and your saving love for us. It boggles our minds to think of what love it was and at what great cost this gift was freely given to us.

Forgive us for all our sin and set us on the path you have for us, blessing us as we go. May we listen to your voice in our hearts and minds and follow where it leads.

Thank you for all your great and undeserved gifts to us. And, bless our studies together so we might come closer to you and our fellow students.

In the name of your son, Jesus our Christ, we pray. Amen.

CHAPTER 7. QUESTIONS

1. Since all have sinned and fallen short of the glory that God has created us to participate in, how did we get in our current condition?

2. What is the meaning of justification? Who needs to be justified?

3. Do we make ourselves holy so the holy God can accept us? Why did you answer as you did?

4. Why is faith in Christ necessary for justification?

5. If justification takes care of past sins does it also take care of future sins? Explain your answer.

6. Can justified Christians sin? What happens then?

7. Does Christian Perfection mean we can see into the future? If not, what does it mean?

8. There are three ways to describe Christian Perfection. What are they?

9. Can we receive Christian Perfection in this life?

CHAPTER 8 Methodist Beliefs (cont.)

Article X—Of Good Works

Although good works, which are the fruits of faith, and follow after justification, cannot put away our sins, and endure the severity of God's judgment, yet are they pleasing and acceptable to God in Christ, and spring out of a true and lively faith, insomuch that by them a lively faith may be as evidently known as a tree is discerned by its fruit. [35]

Article XI—Of Works of Supererogation

Voluntary works—besides, over and above God's commandments—which they call works of supererogation, cannot be taught without arrogancy and impiety. For by them men do declare that they do not only render unto God as much as they are bound to do, but that they do more for his sake than of bounden duty is required, whereas Christ saith plainly: When you have done all that is commanded you, say, We are unprofitable servants. [36]

As they were gathering for their next session the group was having fun.

"You mean to tell me," Todd said to his wife, Melinda "that all the extra work I did for you yesterday doesn't count for anything? Here I thought I was doing a lot of good work."

Melinda said, "It didn't save you, but I was thankful for your help, and you did get an extra scoop of ice cream after dinner."

The others laughed at this exchange and Barb said "the area of good works had always been interesting to me. Some of my Catholic friends look upon good works differently than I do and I'm happy to go over some of the differences and understand it better."

"Girls," Felista said, "there is no way they can do too much."

"Oh boy," replied James.

Shawn said "I like Todd's idea and I would be willing to get an extra scoop of ice cream too."

Felista said, "Sometimes good works really go astray. Two nights ago James thought he'd help by fixing dinner before I got home. However, I didn't know that and I brought home Chinese take out."

"So true," mused James.

---

[35] *The Book of discipline of the United Methodist Church*, 66, 2012
[36] Ibid, 66,

Christians and others have wondered and debated the meaning of good works, who does them and at what stage in the Christian life they can be called good, can they be done apart from Christianity, and what do they have to do with our salvation.

Good works are of several kinds and have different meanings in the Christian life. Good works before justification are not really Christian good works. Society may think they are good, the person performing them may also think they are good, and in fact they may not be bad works at all and done for the common good. However, since they come before justification by faith by grace they cannot be called Christian good works. Since there is no restored relationship with God at this point they cannot have any religious significance as far as salvation is concerned and religious significance is what we are talking about.

Wesley clarifies this for us so well:

> If it be objected, "Nay, but a man, before he is justified, may feed the hungry, or clothe the naked; and these are good works;" the answer is easy: He may do these, even before he is justified; and these are, in one sense, "good works;" they are "good and profitable to men." But it does not follow, that they are, strictly speaking, good in themselves, or good in the sight of God. All truly *good works* (to use the words of our Church) *follow after justification;* and they are therefore good and "acceptable to God in Christ," because they "spring out of a true and living faith." By a parity of reason, *all works done before justification are not good*, in the Christian sense, *forasmuch as they spring not of faith in Jesus Christ;* (though from some kind of faith in God they may spring;...[37]

---

[37] Wesley, *Works*, 5:59

In terms of salvation, good works can only come out of a faith relationship with Christ. If one is truly justified by faith, good works must necessarily be the result. Our life is transformed and it must now bear fruit—different fruit than it has borne before. These works are a natural result of the love which flows through us in our response to the loving and saving God. Because they flow from our grateful and thankful response to what God has done for us through Christ they can be called good works.

These good works do not save us and they do not make us right in God's eyes because salvation is by grace alone by faith alone. However, God is pleased with our loving and joyful response to his love. There is one caveat and this is these good works do flow from justification if there is time in our lives to show them. In fact, if we really are justified by faith these good works must follow as the good fruit comes from the good tree or vine. One case of not having time to show good fruit would be like the case of the thief on the cross who repented, but there was no time for him to do good works. This is what is meant by the caveat mentioned above i.e. they must be time to perform them, for them to grow from our faith.

In another short quote Wesley shows us the importance of fruits in the Christian life because without them Wesley does not think we have really been justified.

> God does undoubtedly command us both to repent, and to bring forth fruits meet for repentance: which if we willingly neglect, we cannot reasonably expect to be justified at all: therefore both repentance, and fruits meet for repentance, are, in some sense, necessary to justification.[38]

Wesley hastens to add these fruits in no way bring about justification because they are necessary only if there is time (one does not die before having the opportunity) because a person may be justified by faith without works if time is lacking.

---

[38] Wesley, *Standard Sermons*, 2:451

As far as supererogation, we Protestants do not believe in them. Since we believe salvation is by grace alone by faith alone, and good works are our response to what God has done for us, it cannot follow that we can provide more good works than God wants or expects for our lives.

It would be impossible for us to perform so many good works we somehow or someway overwhelm God by them. No matter how many they are or how much we give to good works we can never do more for God than he has done for us.

God does not put a limit on good works and say to us if you exceed my expectation for you or for humanity you may bank or keep these good works for later in life or give them to another. We are each to work out our salvation before God with fear and trembling.

It is impossible for us to have good works above and beyond the complete fulfilling of the law and the commandments—only one person did fulfill the law and the commandments and that is God's Son, Jesus our Christ. One might wish we could bank away or put back some good deeds so when we stumble in the future—and we all will stumble and sin in the future—we could just pull out a few good works from the past and be covered. This might be a comforting thought if it was true, but it is not.

We are saved by God's grace and our acceptance of this grace, not by works. Wesley has a tremendous emphasis upon works, but he does not believe we can exceed God's desire for us.

> ...there are no works of supererogation; that we can never do more than our duty; seeing all we have is not our own, but God's; all we can do is due to him. We have not received this or that, or many things only, but every thing from him: Therefore, every thing is his due. He that gives us all, must needs have a right to all: So that if we pay him any thing less than all, we cannot be faithful stewards. And considering, "every man shall receive his own reward, according to his own labour," we cannot be wise stewards unless we labour to the uttermost of our power; not leaving any things undone

which we possibly can do, but putting forth all our strength.[39]

Pastor Bill said, "I'm happy to see the group again, and I'll pass the offering plate right now," which brought a lot of laughs. He said "You are doing a good job reading and keeping up with the studies."

"Study? My eyeballs have gone flat and my brain has gone to mush," said Melinda.

"Piece of cake," responded Shawn.

"I'm happy you can tell we are working hard," said Barb. "Some of us have been studying together during the week."

"Yeah," replied Jim, "you guys are cheating. While we were working or doing other things you gals are drinking coffee, relaxing and having a good time."

"Do you really want to change places with us," said Barb.

"Right on woman, tell is like it is," said Felista. "They can walk in our shoes for a few days and they'll be happy to change back."

"Uh, not really," said James.

Now Pastor Bill told the group they would focus on the sacraments which Methodists and other Protestants celebrate and why we are different from the Roman Catholics.

Article XVI—Of the Sacraments

Sacraments ordained of Christ are not only badges or tokens of Christian men's profession, but rather they are certain signs of grace, and God's good will toward us, by which he doth work invisibly in us, and doth not only quicken, but also strengthen and confirm, our faith in him.

There are two Sacraments ordained of Christ our Lord in the Gospel; that is to say, Baptism and the Supper of the Lord.

Those five commonly called sacraments, that is to say, confirmation, penance, orders, matrimony, and extreme unction, are not to be counted for Sacraments of the Gospel; being such as have partly grown out of the corrupt following of the apostles, and partly are states of life allowed in the Scriptures, but yet have not the like nature of Baptism and the Lord's Supper, because they have not any visible sign or ceremony ordained of God.

---

[39] Wesley, *Works*, 6:148

Sacraments were not ordained of Christ to be gazed upon, or to be carried about; but that we should duly use them. And in such only as worthily receive the same, they have a wholesome effect or operation; but they that receive them unworthily, purchase to themselves condemnation, as St. Paul saith.[40]

Article XVII—Of Baptism

Baptism is not only a sign of profession and mark of difference whereby Christians are distinguished from others that are not baptized; but it is also a sign of regeneration or the new birth. The Baptism of young children is to be retained in the Church.[41]

Article XVIII—Of the Lord's Supper

The Supper of the Lord is not only a sign of the love that Christians ought to have among themselves one to another, but rather is a sacrament of our redemption by Christ's death; insomuch that, to such as rightly, worthily, and with faith receive the same, the bread which we break is a partaking of the body of Christ; and likewise the cup of blessing is a partaking of the blood of Christ.

Transubstantiation, or the change of the substance of bread and wine in the Supper of our Lord, cannot be proved by Holy Writ, but is repugnant to the plain words of Scripture, overthroweth the nature of a sacrament, and hath given occasion to many superstitions

The body of Christ is given, taken, and eaten in the Supper, only after a heavenly and spiritual manner. And the mean whereby the body of Christ is received and eaten in the Supper is faith.

The Sacrament of the Lord's Supper was not by Christ's ordinance reserved, carried about, lifted up, or worshipped.[42]

Article XIX—Of Both Kinds

The cup of the Lord is not to be denied to the lay people; for both the parts of the Lord's Supper, by Christ's ordinance and commandment, ought to be administered to all Christians alike.[43]

---

[40] The *Discipline of the United Methodist Church*, 67, 2012
[41] Ibid, 67
[42] Ibid, 68
[43] The *Discipline of the United Methodist Church*, 68, 2012

Article XX—Of the One Oblation of Christ, Finished upon the Cross

The offering of Christ, once made, is that perfect redemption, propitiation, and satisfaction for all the sins of the whole world, both original and actual; and there is none other satisfaction for sin but that alone. Wherefore the sacrifice of masses, in which it is commonly said that the priest doth offer Christ for the quick and the dead, to have remission of pain or guilt, is a blasphemous fable and dangerous deceit.[44]

After a quick break the group got right into the thick of it.

A. Of The Sacraments

Felista said "I have friends who are Roman Catholics and said they have seven sacraments. Why do we have only two when they have seven? Who determines how many sacraments there are, anyway?"

"The change from 7 to 2 sacraments came about due to the Protestant Reformation, at least that how it is if I remember it correctly," said Barb.

Todd said "I'm glad there are only two because I don't have to remember so many."

"Todd would remember them if his denomination had them," said Shawn. "He would have to remember them so he would."

"The sacraments are an area I am really interested in and am happy we are studying them," said Melinda.

"We want Glenda to be baptized so we were happy to learn more about the meaning of it," said Barb. "We are really looking forward to it and it is good for us to know even more about it with our studies here."

Felista said, "I, uh we had our children christened, or was it baptized?"

Pastor Bill said "we will answer most of these questions in this session. We Methodists, like most of the non-Catholic Christians, believe in two sacraments and they are the Lord's Supper and baptism."

Long after Christ's day the Roman Catholic Church put forth seven sacraments. The seven were made a matter for faith for them in 1500 C.E. Prior to then there were two, at least some of the church

---

[44] Ibid, 68

Fathers thought two was the correct number. There was disagreement as to the exact number of sacraments in the church. However the Church in 1500 C.E. determined that seven were to be called sacraments and made a matter of faith for the Roman Catholics.

Luther, Calvin and others in the Protestant Reformation thought the correct number was two. Luther says "There are, strictly speaking, but two sacraments in the Church of God—baptism and bread; for only in these two do we find both the divinely instituted sign and the promise of forgiveness of sins."[45]

Calvin says it this way:

> In regard to our sacraments, they present Christ the more clearly to us, the more familiarly he has been manifested to man, ever since he was exhibited by the Father, truly as he had been promised. For Baptism testifies that we are washed and purified; the Supper of the Eucharist that we are redeemed. Ablution is figured by water, satisfaction by blood. Both are found in Christ, who, as John says "came by water and blood;" that is, to purify and redeem. Of this the Spirit of God also is a witness.[46]

We and the Roman Catholics say a sacrament must be instituted by Christ. We also agree a sacrament has to have form and matter. For example, the matter in baptism is water and the form is the words of consecration or "I baptize you in the name of the Father, the Son, and the Holy Spirit."

We have a problem with some of their sacraments or what they call a sacrament because we do not see a form in confirmation and extreme unction, likewise we do not see matter or form of divine institution in penance or matrimony.

We believe the sacraments are not magical so by merely repeating them, somehow something of significance is done for us. We

---

[45] Luther, Martin, *A Compend of Luther's Theology*, 163-4
[46] Calvin, John, *Institutes of the Christian Religion*, 2:507

must also believe and be ready to receive the sacrament. To make it clear, the mere saying of the words, or repeating the words does nothing; what is important is the blessing which God gives us because of partaking of the sacraments rightly.

B. Of Baptism

> Go therefore and make disciples of all nations, baptizing them in the name of the Father and of the Son and of the Holy Spirit, and teaching them to obey everything that I have commanded you. And remember, I am with you always, to the end of the age." Matthew 28:19-20

Though Jesus did not baptize we have the command from Him to baptize.

In our church, unlike some other churches we sprinkle, pour or immerse—all three. The reason we will perform baptism in any of these ways is we do not see where the Scripture tells us to perform it one way or another.

The matter of the sacrament is water, which is peculiarly appropriate because of water's cleaning properties. The Scriptures are not clear on what method was used. However it is performed it is done in the name of the Father, the Son and the Holy Spirit.

As Wesley says:

> To sum up all, the manner of baptizing (whether by dipping or sprinkling) is not determined in Scripture. There is no command for one rather than the other. There is no example from which we can conclude for dipping rather than sprinkling. There are probable examples of both; and both are equally contained in the natural meaning of the word.[47]

---

[47] Wesley, *Works*, 10:190

The sacrament of baptism initiates us into a covenant with God. Baptism was instituted by Christ who alone has the power to do so. It took the place of circumcision which is found in the Jewish faith.

The benefits of baptism include the washing away of original sin. We are all born under the guilt of Adam's sin and this cleanses us from that disease. The child may not have sinned in any way but because we are children of Adam we participate in this disease. The child may not have been able to sin on their own yet so the only sin washed away for babies has to be original sin.

By baptism we also enter into a covenant with God. This covenant gives us a new heart and spirit and God will be our God.

We are likewise admitted into the church and are then members of Christ who is head of the Church. We have then a vital union with Christ, receiving his grace and because we are in the church we share in the privileges and the promises Christ has made to the church.

Another benefit is we who were outside the loving relationship with God have become children of God. Because we are now children of God we are heirs of heaven.

Baptism will be with us as long as there is a church and those who are not in the church are seeking entry.

We believe in the baptism of children whereas some other Protestants do not. There are several reasons why we have come to this conclusion.

As stated earlier, if children belong to the human race after Adam, they are infected with the disease of original sin which he has passed down to all. Baptism washes away this disease.

The children of Abraham and the children from them down to this day are included in the gospel covenant. This covenant was a gospel of faith and the fruit of that faith was obedience. In this covenant children were obliged by what they did not know to the same faith and obedience as Abraham. They are likewise today entitled to all the benefits and promises of the covenant.

If infants should come to Christ, if they are capable of being admitted into the church, and can be sacramentally dedicated to Christ, they are proper subjects of baptism.

The apostles baptized infants and infants have been baptized in the Christian church in all places and in all ages. Not one Christian church in the early days of the church refused to baptize children when they were brought to the church for baptism.

There is no need for a second baptism. Once you have been baptized you can forever look back to your baptism. Those who were baptized as children or babies can at confirmation now or even at a later date, retake the vows of baptism without having to be baptized again. Some may think being baptized as a child is something called christening, or naming of the child. Baptism is baptism and once is enough. Double, triple or quadruple baptism adds nothing. You can always look back to your baptism and renew your vows and be comforted that God works through your baptism.

The sacrament of baptism follows and is built upon the sacrament of circumcision. Children were circumcised on the eighth (8th) day, so baptism, which performs many of the same things as circumcision, should be available to children.

Wesley summarizes it so well:

> If outward baptism be generally, in an ordinary way, necessary to salvation, and infants may be saved as well as adults, nor ought we to neglect any means of saving them; if our Lord commands such to come, to be brought unto him, and declares, "Of such is the kingdom of heaven;" if infants are capable of making a covenant, or having a covenant made for them by others, being included in Abraham's covenant, (which was a covenant of faith, an evangelical covenant,) and never excluded by Christ; if they have a right to be members of the Church, and were accordingly members of the Jewish; if, suppose our Lord had designed to exclude them from baptism, he must have expressly forbidden his Apostles to baptize them, (which none dares to affirm he did,) since otherwise they would do it of course, according to the universal practice of their nation; if it is highly probably they did so, even from the letter of Scripture, because they frequently baptized whole households,

and it would be strange if there were no children among them; if the whole Church of Christ, for seventeen hundred years together, baptized infants, and were never opposed till the last century but one, by some not very holy men in Germany; lastly, if there are such inestimable benefits conferred in baptism, the washing away the guilt of original sin, the engrafting us into Christ, by making us members of his Church, and thereby giving us a right to all the blessings of the gospel; it follows, that infants may, yea, ought to be baptized, and that none ought to hinder them.[48]

C. Of the Lord's Supper

While they were eating, Jesus took a loaf of bread, and after blessing it he broke it, gave it to the disciples, and said "Take, eat: this is my body." Then he took a cup, and after giving thanks he gave it to them, saying, "Drink from it, all of you; for this is my blood of the covenant, which is poured out for many for the forgiveness of sins. I tell you, I will never again drink of this fruit of the vine until that day when I drink it new with you in my Father's kingdom." Matthew 26:26-29

To Wesley and to those who follow his lead, the Lord's Supper is central to the life of the church. We discussed growth in grace and the Christian life when we discussed Christian Perfection. As Methodists we have a great belief in growing in grace. The Lord's Supper is a sacrament in which God's grace is given to his children.

---

[48] Wesley, *Works*, 10:198

In parts of our church communion is partaken of only once a quarter. In our area it is monthly, mainly on the first Sunday in the month. However, for Wesley it was much more frequent. He believes we have a duty of constant communion.

One reason we should think of constant communion is that it is the command of Christ. The bread and wine are commanded to be received in remembrance of his death until the end of the world.

Another reason we should consider the frequency of the Lord's Supper is because of the benefits we receive by following his command. These benefits include the forgiveness of our sins and the strengthening, nourishing, and refreshing of our souls. The grace of God which we receive through partaking of the Supper confirms to us that our sins are indeed forgiven. As our bodies are strengthened by the bread and wine so our souls are strengthened by the tokens of Christ's body and blood—it is the food of our souls.

> If, therefore, we have any regard for the plain command of Christ, if we desire the pardon of our sins, if we wish for strength to believe, to love and obey God, then we should neglect no opportunity of receiving the Lord's Supper; then we must never turn our backs on the feast which our Lord has prepared for us. We must neglect no occasion, which the good providence of God affords us, for this purpose. This is the true rule: So often are we to receive as God gives us opportunity. Whoever, therefore, does not receive, but goes from the holy table, when all things are prepared, either does not understand his duty, or does not care for the dying command of his Saviour, the forgiveness of his sins, the strengthening of his soul, and the refreshing it with the hope of glory.[49]

---

[49] Wesley, *Works*, 7:148

Pastor Bill said, "This is why St. Mark church has the Lord's Supper every Sunday year round."

Christ is really present in the sacrament and he gives his grace to those who partake. Though we receive this sacrament through faith, this faith is not to be construed as making us worthy to receive him. What we bring to the table is knowledge of our unworthiness and a conviction we can trust his promise to be present when we receive the elements.

Our church believes the Lord's Supper gives us three ways of understanding how the Supper can move us forward on the path of salvation.

The first is the Lord's Supper represents the sufferings of Christ. In this way we understand it as a memorial. It is, though, not only a reminder of something which has happened in the past, but God also uses it now to present to us again the sacrifice of Christ in the Supper so our faith may be energized and we may receive the merits of Christ by his sacrifice for the sins of the whole world.

The second is Christ is really present in the Supper. By eating the bread and drinking the cup which are the outward and visible means through which God graciously gives spiritual grace, and we receive righteousness, peace, and joy through the Holy Spirit.

The Lord's Supper can give to the believer new graces to grow in the Christian life but it can also lead the non-believer or initiate into an acceptance of Christ.

The third is involved in our future in the sense of partaking of the Supper can prepare us for our final destiny. Not only does it prepare us for heaven it is a pledge of the heavenly banquet with Christ.

As Protestants we believe the bread and wine do not physically become the body and blood of Jesus. The Scriptures say Jesus said this is my body, not the bread has been turned into my body. In fact, it is called the bread even after it has been consecrated.

Truly the mystical relation which the bread and wine or grape juice have by consecrating them is enough for them to be called the body and blood of Christ. In fact it is the usual way the Scriptures refer to the sacrament by the name of the elements. Examples of this are the Scriptures calling God's covenant with the Jews, circumcision, and in like manner the discussion of killing and preparing the Passover lamb stands for the Passover.

Some books on the sacraments for the United Methodist Church by Gayle C. Felton are listed in the bibliography and available from Cokesbury.

D. Both

We, like most Protestants administer both of the elements, the bread and wine or grape juice, to the communicants. Jesus himself gave both the bread and wine to his disciples and we see no need to handle the sacraments differently than how Christ gave it to them.

> An evil practice attending this evil doctrine is, the depriving the laity of the cup in the Lord's Supper. It is acknowledged by all, that our Lord instituted and delivered this sacrament in both kinds; giving the wine as well as the bread to all that partook of it; and that it continued to be so delivered in the Church of Rome for above a thousand years. And yet, notwithstanding this, the Church of Rome now forbids the people to drink of the cup! A more insolent and barefaced corruption cannot easily be conceived![50]

Todd asked "why did the Catholic Church then change from giving both of the elements and go to giving only one?"

Pastor Bill said "The church gave a variety of reasons for this change and they are the blood of Christ might be spilt upon the ground, some may not like the taste or smell of wine, there may be a scarcity of wine in some areas of the world, and it would show those who deny Christ is in both elements are in error."

"I like our way of communion better," Jim said, "because it seems to be in line with the Scriptures, doesn't it?"

"Isn't it something, to be doing the same thing people have been doing for about twenty centuries," said Melinda.

---

[50] Wesley, *Works*, 10, 152

E. One Oblation

Though there are some who believe Christ is given again, or his body is broken again for our sins in the sacrament, we believe the sacrifice given by Christ on the cross was once given and never needs to be given again.

This was put in to differentiate us from the Roman Catholics who believe Christ is sacrificed again in the mass.

> But if the same Christ is offered in the mass as was on the cross, and that unbloody sacrifice is alike propitiatory as the bloody, there is then a repetition of the same sacrifice, and he is daily offered. And what is to say, the one was bloody and the other is unbloody, when the unbloody is of the same virtue, and is applied to the same end, as the bloody? So that, as, if Christ had again been bloodily offered up, there had been a repetition of that sacrifice; so there is a repetition of it when he is offered up unbloodily. To have then a perfect sacrifice daily repeated, and a sacrifice without suffering, and a propitiation and remission without blood, are alike irreconcilable to the Apostle.[51]

---

[51] Wesley, *Works*, 10, 120-1

SCRIPTURE

Then he took a cup, and after giving thanks he said, "Take this and divide it among yourselves; for I tell you that from now on I will not drink of the fruit of the vine until the kingdom of God comes." Then he took a loaf of bread, and when he had given thanks he broke it and gave it to them saying "This is my body, which is given for you. Do this in remembrance of me." And he did the same with the cup after supper, saying, "This cup that is poured out for you is the new covenant in my blood. (Luke 22:17-20)

PRAYER

Our Heavenly Father who has graciously and lovingly sent your Son into the world so we who were living in sin, estranged, apart from, trusting in our own selves and our own little gods, might instead be able to enter back into a saving relationship with you. We give you thanks for these mighty works.

Be with our families and loved ones and all those who are called Christians and who participate in the sacraments given to us by the Son of God. Create in us more love for you and for each other, thinking not primarily of those things which separate us but those which tightly bind us each to the other.

May our studies be fruitful and our fellowship be full of love and understanding. In the name of Christ we ask. Amen.

CHAPTER 8. QUESTIONS

1. What do we mean by the term good works? There are undoubtedly two definitions or understanding of good works, the common one that the world can see and appreciate and the one that God sees and appreciates. What is the difference between them?

2. What is the relationship between good works and salvation? And where do we differ from our Roman Catholic Christian friends?

3. What is considered a work of supererogation? Do we as Protestants believe in them? Why or why not?

4. Name the sacraments that we have as Protestant Methodists? Why does the number of our sacraments differ from our Catholic Christian friends?

5. Sacraments have to have form and matter. What is the form and the matter in baptism?

6. What is the correct form of baptism—sprinkling, pouring, or dipping? Why do you think that this is the correct form?

7. What is the significance of baptism for us today?

8. If you have once been baptized, when you join the United Methodist Church do you have to be rebaptized or baptized again? Why?

9. How frequent should you participate in the Lord's Supper? Why?

10. In what spirit should you come to the table of our Lord?

11. Why do we United Methodists believe in partaking of the two elements in the Lord's Supper and some others such as the Roman Catholics do not?

12. What three ways do we believe partaking of the Lord's Supper can move us forward to ultimate salvation?

CHAPTER 9 Methodist Beliefs (cont.)

Article XIII—Of the Church

The visible church of Christ is a congregation of faithful men in which the pure Word of God is preached, and the Sacraments duly administered according to Christ's ordinance, in all those things that of necessity are requisite to the same.[52]

The study group assembled and discussed what had happened over the past week. Jim and Barb, Shawn and Diane, had a hamburger and wiener roast for the families. Pastor Bill and his wife were there as were Todd and Melinda and Felista and James. Then they settled down to watch the local football team, the University of South Alabama, on TV. South had won the game but not until after a hard fought struggle, so they were still talking about the game when Pastor Bill joined in and told them one of their children is attending South Alabama and they were Jaguar fans also.

The discussion of the day was on and about the church.

Diane said "I know the church is really not the building but is really the people who worship there, isn't that right." This statement opened the door for a lot of discussion and ideas.

"I think you are absolutely right, Diane," replied Jim.

Shawn answered, "She always thinks she is right" and he hurriedly added, "And she normally is."

In his opening remarks about the church, Pastor Bill said about every Christian group would agree with this statement in the Articles of the church, but they begin to disagree as soon as they begin to define what they mean by it and whether or not anything else should be added to this definition.

Shawn said, "We could then skip this area if it is that simple and clear."

Pastor Bill said, "This doctrine is a necessary one and all will become clear soon.

The term or word the "church" is kind of a weasel word in one sense and because the word can have many meanings. Though it can be both a building and a group of people we will discuss the church as a group of people who are united together.

---

[52] *The Book of Discipline of the United Methodist Church*, 66, 2012

The church can also mean a small group of people up to a large group of people. It is not limited by size. The church is also not limited to location as if all churches had to be in St. Louis, or in the United States, and not in other locations as well. We can also talk about the churches in our city, or any other city, or state, or area of the world.

When we talk about the church in general we mean the catholic or universal church and not just one denomination or part of the Christian church. This is the entire group of believers' in Christ, worldwide. However, when we do this we have to be careful because even though it includes people from all over the earth they have and must have certain things in common.

This group, composed of people throughout the world, has one spirit. This spirit moves and is within all the members of the group. Some call this the Holy Spirit or having the spirit which was in Christ. Others consider more closely the spiritual gifts which are given to members of the church.

We who have this spirit also live with one hope, the hope of immortality. We know we will die but to die is not to be eternally lost. Our hope carries beyond the grave. Because Jesus has been raised from the dead we can also live in hope of doing so because of the promises of God, and God is faithful in fulfilling his promises.

Just as there is one spirit in all and one hope, there is one Lord who is over all. The kingdom is not divided between competing gods or warriors. There is only one and he has set up his kingdom in our hearts and reigns we who have this hope. To follow him and his commandments is our glory and our joy.

We have one faith; we are not divided in our loyalties. This faith we have talked about before, this faith is the free gift from God and it is the ground of our hope. This is the faith which draws from us the exclamation "my Lord and my God." It is the faith which allows us to say with St. Paul the life I now live, I live by faith in the Son of God, who loved me and gave himself for me.

All of these "ones," we have just discussed and yet there is an additional "one." For us there is one baptism which is the outward sign given to us by Christ to show the inward and spiritual grace he gives constantly to his church. It is likewise the way this faith and hope are given to those who diligently seek him.

Finally, there is one God and Father of all—not multiple, not maybe—who has given us the Spirit of adoption allowing us to boldly proclaim him as Father; and God witnesses to us and our spirits reply we are the children of God.

This then is the catholic or universal church in its shortest definition, all the people in the universe who God has called out of the world to be one body and united by one spirit whereby we have one faith, one hope, one baptism—one God and Father of all who is above all, through all and in all.

Wesley states the necessity of holiness and action on the part of the church.

> The Church is called *holy*, because it *is* holy, because every member thereof is holy, though in different degrees, as He that called them is holy. How clear is this! If the Church, as to the very essence of it, is a body of believers, no man that is not a Christian believer can be a member of it. If this whole body be animated by one spirit, and endued with one faith, and one hope of their calling; then he who has not that spirit, and faith, and hope, is no member of this body.[53]

Wesley was a true ecumenical long before the present interest in ecumenism. Perhaps because of his work within the Church of England and his clear vision of what church life is and should be, he was able to separate the important from the unimportant.

We Methodists have not been sticklers for any particular order of worship. We have center pulpits and divided ones. We have pastors who scrupulously follow the church year with colors, robes etc. and we have those who preach in blue jeans. You could say we run from High Church and formal services to Low Church and informal services. There is a place for almost every type of service for those who want them.

We have an Episcopal form of government in our church but with our multiple conferences and committees with laity equally represented it could easily be called government by committee.

---

[53] Wesley, *Works*, 6, 400

Looked at another way, the church has to have three elements in order for it to be the visible Christian Church. The first thing a church must have is a living faith. There cannot be a church of any kind, visible or invisible, which does not have a living faith.

The second element is the preaching of the Word of God because otherwise the faith would tend to become minimal and might even cease altogether.

The third element is where the sacraments are duly administered because these sacraments are the usual means by which God increases our faith.

It is interesting to note the importance of our agreement with this definition. Even though most Christians agree with this definition so far, it is the emphasis which is placed on one or the other which tends to separate us.

If we place our emphasis upon living faith we are in the group of churches which are normally called Free Churches.

If we place our emphasis upon the preaching and hearing the word of God we find ourselves with the Protestant group of churches. In this case, living faith and due administration of the sacraments arise from preaching the Word of God and its reception by the people.

If we place our emphasis upon the due administration of the sacraments and go one step more and add the unbroken succession of the ministry, we are in the Catholic group.

Wesley himself speaks of the church of God or the church in general or the catholic or universal church in the following ways, taking as his reference Paul's letter to the Ephesians.

There is one God and Father of all that have been adopted and cry out from their hearts "Father." As Wesley says:

> "What is the Church?" The catholic or universal Church is, all the persons in the universe whom God hath so called out of the world as to entitle them to the preceding character; as to be "one body," united by "one Spirit; having "one faith, one hope, one baptism; one God and Father of all, who is above all, and through all, and in them all."[54]

---

[54] Wesley, *Works*, 6, 395-6

Wesley does have a problem with the definition of the church if we limit it to being where the pure word of God is preached and the sacraments are duly administered. The reason he gives for not fully accepting this definition is he cannot put outside the Church catholic all those churches in which the pure word of God is not preached and those in which the sacraments are not duly administered. He thinks this would cut off many who are really Christian.

If he followed this definition totally he thought the Roman Catholic Church would not be considered Christian and he could not stand for such an unnecessary and illegitimate limitation. He has no problem with them being Christian and in fact he would happily receive them into the Church of England.

Article XIV—Of Purgatory

The Romish doctrine concerning purgatory, pardon, worshipping and adoration, as well of images as of relics, and also invocation of saints, is a fond thing, vainly invented, and grounded upon no warrant of Scripture, but repugnant to the Word of God.[55]

We will handle some of the others in short order because they are not Methodist beliefs or they do not require much discussion.

For instance, we do not believe in purgatory which is the place Roman Catholics believe people go who are in grace but need to be purged further for their sins before they can be accepted into heaven.

We cannot find such to be in Scripture or in the ancient fathers of the church. Many Scriptures tell us if God justifies us who is to condemn. Think of the thief on the cross who was promised to be in paradise with Jesus that day. You would think such a person would need to be purged but Jesus does not. John 5:24 says it for us: "Very truly, I tell you, anyone who hears my word and believes him who sent me has eternal life, and does not come under judgment, but has passed from death to life."

---

[55] *Book of Discipline of the United Methodist Church*, 66-7

Article XV—Of Speaking in the Congregation in Such a Tongue as the People Understand

It is a thing plainly repugnant to the Word of God, and the custom of the primitive church, to have public prayer in the church, or to minister the Sacraments, in a tongue not understood by the people.[56]

This is pretty self explanatory. If you cannot understand the preached Word of God of what use is it to you? The preacher or minister may know what he is talking about but if the congregation cannot understand how is it of value to them? To administer the sacraments or pray to God and not understand what God is gracefully giving us is of no use to us.

"You know, when I was younger, said Felista "I went to a church with one of my friends and they got excited and talked in a way I had no idea what they were saying and I got embarrassed."

Barb said "some people believe such talking is important and if you can't talk that way you really don't count. I however don't believe that way and anyway if you can't understand what someone is saying it really doesn't mean much to you or anybody else, for that matter."

"I do want to understand what's going on in the service," said Shawn. It makes no sense to me to have something going on or somebody saying something I do not understand."

"Me too," said Todd.

Article XXII—Of the Rites and Ceremonies of Churches

It is not necessary that rites and ceremonies should in all places be the same, or exactly alike; for they have been always different, and may be changed according to the diversity of countries, times, and men's manners, so that nothing be ordained against God's Word. Whosoever, through his private judgment, willingly and purposely doth openly break the rites and ceremonies of the church to which he belongs, which are not repugnant to the Word of God, and are ordained and approved by common authority, ought to be rebuked openly, that others may fear to do the like, as one that offendeth against the common order of the church, and woundeth the consciences of weak brethren.

Every particular church may ordain, change, or abolish rites and ceremonies, so that all things may be done to edification.[57]

---

[56] *Book of Discipline of the United Methodist Church*, 67
[57] Ibid, 69

The United Methodist Church is not bound to follow any particular rite or ceremony. We are free to choose among many as long as they are not against the Word of God. In our hymnbooks and books of worship are plenty of suggested ones which may be followed as well as others. We are not to just willy-nilly make up our own forms or rites without justification from the Word of God or at least not contrary to it.

In part here Wesley is telling us religion or Christianity does not reside in the outer form or in the rite properly performed. Real or true religion is not a matter of outward forms or ritual observances. True religion or Christianity is a matter of the heart.

No matter how decent, significant, or expressive a form or ritual is we should never confuse it with religion. Christianity is so much bigger than all of these. Christianity is not even a matter of orthodoxy or unorthodoxy or of opinions right or wrong. One can be ultimately correct on all points of theology, opinions etc., theology is not the heart; it is only the finite understanding of humanity.

The religion of the heart is religion. Christianity as such is righteousness, peace, and joy in the Holy Spirit.

In the two great commandments, to love God and neighbor, God asks us to love him and to let him reign in our hearts alone, without a rival. He is our strength, or defender, and the one we trust.

The second part of the great commandment is to love your neighbor as you do yourself. Good will, affection, a desire to prevent evil, and working for our neighbors good is the way we are to treat our neighbor as well as ourselves. Having this love is fulfilling the law and thus it is righteousness.

True religion even goes further because it implies we will be happy as well as holy. The peace of God can and will be given to us. This peace does away with fear, doubt, and uncertainty. The Spirit of God bears witness with our spirits that we are children of God.

True religion is not only righteousness and peace, it includes joy. We rejoice in God's work because we have been brought from or changed from alienated sinners to lovers of God and it is God's work, not ours, his grace and not our hard work. We are happy because we know God has promised these to us and God keeps his promises.

You see being a Christian is not a matter of correct beliefs, though they are not unimportant; being a Christian is not a matter of religious observances and correct performances of them, though they have their place; being a Christian is a matter of the heart and what or who is in it, this is what is important!

"Now I like this concept," said Barb. "My theology may not be complete or always clear but I'm not judged by that."

"I like it too," replied Felista. "I work hard to understand but even then at times I know there are limits to what I understand."

"Amen to that," said James, and the others laughed at the humor.

SCRIPTURE

Paul, called to be an apostle of Christ Jesus by the will of God, and our brother Sosthenes, To the church of God that is in Corinth, to those who are sanctified in Christ Jesus called to be saints, together with all those who in every place call on the name of our Lord Jesus Christ, both their Lord and ours:

Grace to you and peace from God our Father and the Lord Jesus Christ.

(1 Corinthians 1:1-3)

PRAYER

Our Father, Creator and Redeemer of your creation, who out of love for us sent your son to live among us and show us your love and mighty works on our behalf, we give thanks to the many blessings and grace given to us.

We give thanks for the church, the church whose head is Jesus our Christ and whose body is we who believe and follow him and we are happy to be included as members. We thank you for all churches dedicated to him and especially for our local church.

May our thoughts, reading, and studies be fruitful in gaining further knowledge and love of our God and Lord Jesus Christ.

Bless our fellowship this day. In the name of Jesus was ask it. Amen.

CHAPTER 9. QUESTIONS

1. What different meanings may the term "church" have?

2. What are the common things which must be present in any church?

3. What are the three elements the church must have?

4. What do we believe about purgatory?

5. What do we believe about speaking in tongues in the church?

6. Do all Methodist churches have to have the same rites? Give reasons for your answer.

7. Do all Methodist churches follow the same ceremonies? Give reasons for your answer.

8. What do we mean by the term "true religion?"

CHAPTER 10 Now That I am Joining the Church, What Should I do?

The group gathered again and discussed what they had finished and what they had yet to cover.

Diane stated, "I enjoyed the time devoted to beliefs of the Methodist Church because I am from another denomination and was unsure about what Methodists believed. There is a lot in common between my old church and this one. There are only a few things which are a little different and I like them."

"I was interested in the breadth of the Methodist Church, how there were high churches and more informal churches," replied Melinda. "This allows people to choose what style of service they feel comfortable with."

Barb said "Even though I was a Methodist when I was a girl it was good to learn more about our beliefs because I really didn't know all of them or why we believed some of them."

James, one of the quiet ones in the group spoke up, "I agree with what we have been talking about and am happy Felista and I decided to attend these sessions."

Pastor Bill said, "Since we have now finished the history and beliefs we will conclude our study by asking the question 'If I am joining the United Methodist Church, what do the church and God expect me to do now?'"

The outline for the answer to this question is given in the ritual used to bring new members into the church and transferring members in from other services which we will use when you will come into the church. Those who are coming from another denomination will be asked one extra question and that is "as members of Christ's universal church will you be loyal to the United Methodist Church, and do all in your power to strengthen its ministries?" The key question that you all will be asked is "as members of Saint Mark United Methodist Church, will you faithfully participate in its ministries by your prayers, your presence, your gifts, your service and your witness?"[58]

He said, "Why don't we now explore our participation in these ministries?"

---

[58] *Book of Discipline of the United Methodist Church,*

A. Prayers

The first thing you should do as a member of the church is to pray for the ministries of the church. This would include our local church as well as the entire United Methodist Church. Our church, St. Mark, ministers to the congregation and to those outside our congregation. Especially pray for your pastor and their family.

Ministering to our congregation is very important because without a strong congregation and strong support from the congregation we cannot effectively minister to those outside the church.

Some of the ministries to our congregation are our worship services and Sunday School program. Then there are the children's programs and the youth programs. Beyond these are the classes we provide for our adult members such as this one, along with the additional courses we have each year. There are also special ones which include various Bible study classes and the excellent classes put on by the United Methodist Women.

This educational and nurturing effort is fundamental for our mission which is so important for our church and which include our Food Pantry programs providing food and other help to the poor, the glazed grace approach which provides free coffee and donuts to harried people on Friday's, the many missions which come from the payment of our connectional funds, and help provide resources to the mission endeavors of the United Methodist Church..

Here in our local church we are also very excited about the possibilities of the new worship service which we talked about earlier and how we can offer additional ministries to our area. There are probably several others I have omitted but these give you some idea of what I am talking about.

Prayer undergirds each of these program ministries. Without prayer and lifting these ministries to God and our consideration of them, we would not be able to keep these ministries going.

Prayer is also a means of grace for each of us as individual Christians. As important as prayer is for the ministries of our congregation and missions of our congregation, prayers are extremely important for each of us as Christians because this is one of the means by which God can and does communicate with us.

Often people ask how to pray and what we should pray about. Jesus taught his disciples a prayer when they asked him. You remember the Lord's Prayer, don't you? Let's pray it now.

> Our Father, who art in heaven, hallowed be thy name. Thy kingdom come, thy will be done on earth as it is in heaven. Give us this day our daily bread. And forgive us our trespasses, as we forgive those who trespass against us. And lead us not into temptation, but deliver us from evil. For thine is the kingdom, and the power, and the glory, forever. Amen.

This prayer itself is instructive, teaching us what Jesus thought we should consider in our prayers with God. I say prayers "with" because we are not engaging in a one way conversation. God listens and answers. As Thomas one of my friends says "it is so easy to forget that prayer is a conversation, not a recitation." Sometimes we are aware of the answers quickly, sometimes it takes us awhile to hear his answers, sometimes it takes a long time for us to understand.

The Lord's Prayer begins with our thinking about God. We call him "Father" which is a term used for closeness to him and in turn suggests we are his children. We are therefore in the family of God and can indeed call him Father. We know what the best human fathers can be like. This is our Heavenly Father, so there has to be much more loving and concern coming from him than could ever come from our earthly fathers, as good as they might be. We can boldly and happily proclaim him as Father and us as his sons and daughters.

Heaven can also signify God is in a place where we are not. This is likewise true because God is not just near, he is more than near, and he is the creator of us all. We can participate in this heaven if we will accept it but we are allowed to reject it as well.

Remember the Psalmist who wrote there is nowhere we can go to get away from God because God is always with us, no matter what we do? You see we can have a foretaste of heaven here and now because we can know God here and be aware of his presence. Just a bit of heaven here on earth for us and which will be even greater when we have joined him after this life is through.

Heaven can mean many things to us. One of the most meaningful is the concept that heaven is where we can be in close relationship with our loving heavenly Father and participate in enjoying each other.

Next we say God's name is to be hallowed. God's name is to be kept holy because God is holy. We praise God and by extension we can praise him for all his attributes of love, kindness, mercy, justice, righteousness—all the wonderful ways we have found God relating to us.

We next ask for God's kingdom to come and his will to be done here as well as in heaven.

In heaven God's will is always done, not by overpowering with his authority but by God's love which is over all and in all.

God's kingdom comes on earth and is already breaking into earth in the hearts and lives of his followers because he is in them and they are in him and as such it is where God rules.

Where God's rule is there is his kingdom and though his rule and kingdom are in heaven his kingdom is likewise here on earth in the hearts and lives of his followers.

It is only at this point, after praising God for the wonders of his love and other attributes and asking for his kingdom to come within our hearts does Jesus turn to the physical needs of human beings.

We pray for bread. It is food to eat but we can further expand its meaning to clothes to wear to protect our bodies and the other necessities of life. Jesus asks for basic, he did not say banquet. Bread is basic whereas banquet is not. Jesus asks for the necessities not the niceties of life.

Then Jesus prays for forgiveness of our sins. Though some have separated the next phrase from this one I prefer to keep them together because I believe they belong together.

We ask God to forgive us our sins as we forgive those who have sinned against us. We are to be like our heavenly Father who has made it possible for all our sins to be forgiven. We are to forgive others for their sins against us as well.

It is not enough to just seek forgiveness from God we are to forgive those who have sinned against us as well. In fact the words are forgive us as we forgive others. How difficult and challenging this is. We are to be forgiven in the same manner and extent as we forgive others.

This is not an easy saying nor is it easy to do. As sons and daughters of our Heavenly Father we are to be like him and do as he says and he forgives us for all our sins and not just the sins of "nice" people or people like us. He has worked through the Son to forgive us all of all our sins. We must forgive and we can forgive because we are children of God and he has granted us the grace to be able to do it.

Lead us not into temptation or do not let us fall into temptation. Keep us from falling into temptation by allowing us to remain in his love and allow his love to be expressed through us. Do not let us fall away from this joyful, loving relationship with God.

By all means deliver us from any evil which would pursue us or which we would pursue. Keep us from evil, save us from evil. Do not allow evil to take over our lives.

And, why do we pray all this? We pray this because God is the kingdom, the power and the glory forever. Amen.

When we join the church and therefore want to come closer to God and improve on our relationship with Him, we can either say we have now done everything we need to do or we can use the means of grace God has provided for us in order to come closer to Him and through which he can lead us. Christianity is not an accomplished thing. We cannot say I am a church member and therefore I have attained all which is necessary. You have seen this concept is false many times as we studied our beliefs.

Jesus himself in the Sermon on the Mount, tells us to ask and it will be given to us, seek and we will find, and knock and it will be opened to us. This means we must be persistent in our use of the means of grace so we can have a stronger relationship with God, one which is caring and meaningful for us.

If this is not enough reason for our prayers, Jesus goes further and says we are imperfect and sinners, but if a child of ours is hungry, will we give him a stone rather than food? Again, if our child asks us for a fish will we give him a snake? Jesus says if we would not do such a thing why would God not give and answer our requests for His love? There are things we need not ask for but anything which makes or helps us grow in Christian understanding or the Christian life is certainly something God surely will give if we just ask after it. If it is outside the loving fellowship between us—God, others and us—it is questionable to ask for it. Such a thing might be to receive a gift of $1,000,000 from an anonymous donor. Will such a gift further your relationship with God? Will this gift offer you saving grace? I think not. But, if it has to do with growing in grace or Christian love for God or for others, this is a different story.

Don't think you can't tell God about a problem or a need of yours or somebody else's because God already knows about the problem. Certainly God is not dumb or deaf or blind. He knows. But by His grace he wants us to talk over these problems with Him. He enjoys our conversations and the relationship growing from our rich prayer life.

One other thing we should discuss is when we pray our minds will wander. Don't berate yourself when they do, just bring yourself back to God and start praying and loving him again.

There is a story about Martin Luther who told his congregation no one could say the Lord's Prayer without their minds wandering. He said he would give his carriage to anyone who could pray the Lord's Prayer without having his mind wander, to which one of his parishioners said he could do it. Luther and the parishioner got together and the parishioner started praying fervently, but right in the middle of the prayer he opened one eye and asked "Do I get the horses too?" Obviously he didn't get the carriage either. Just return to your loving conversation with God because God knows our frailties and will be pleased we have come back to him.

Barb asked "How about praying for others. If God is aware of their problem can't he handle it without me bringing it up?"

Pastor Bill said, "God already knows of the problems but He loves your concern about your neighbor and love for your neighbor. God may find a way to help your neighbor and sometimes the help may even come from you but sometimes it may come from a totally different source. The more people who are praying and the more people who are aware of a need or concern, allow multiple ways for God to use our hands and our feet for His work. Never doubt this truth, God wants to hear your concerns for your family, friends, and neighbors.

Remember God is within us as well as without us, He is over us and under us, He is on our right side and on our left. The nice thing is our prayers can be silent, because God is within and He hears them.

Our prayers can be verbal and out loud as when we pray with our family in thankfulness for His grace and for our food, and clothing. Our prayers can be about ourselves as we have problems and concerns, and they can concern others as we become aware of problems and challenges they are facing. God is not limited by space because you can pray for a relative or friend who might be far away but they, too, are not outside the love of God and His ability to be with them.

Todd said "I didn't know prayers or praying was so important. I've just prayed on occasion and didn't feel the need or necessity for more until now."

"Not only that, I didn't realize praying was a means of grace, a way God and we could get together in love and God's grace could be given to me through prayer," responded Jim.

"This puts a whole new light on the children saying their prayers at night, doesn't it" asked Melinda.

"It sure does," answered Diane, "and I never thought of it as a means of grace for them also."

Pastor Bill said, "There are other means of grace also such as reading the Scripture and the Lord's Supper. Reading the Scriptures or attending Bible study classes allows God to speak to us through His Word. We learn more about Him and His love for us as well as His desire for us to love Him and our fellow humans. As we grow in the Christian life, God continues to lead us and provide new and fresh insights and understanding through His Holy Book."

God uses our reading of the Scripture to confirm and increase true wisdom, not as the world thinks of it but as God gives it. Reading and studying the Scriptures are good both for the believer and those who are not sure but who are seeking something. God can use our earnest searches to deliver his grace to us.

Jesus also told and tells us to partake of the Lord's Supper. It is the new covenant in his blood. As Wesley so aptly said:

> Is not the eating of that bread, and the drinking of that cup, the outward, visible means whereby God conveys into our souls all that spiritual grace, that righteousness, and peace, and joy in the Holy Ghost, which were purchased by the body of Christ once broken, and the blood of Christ once shed for us? Let all, therefore, who truly desire the grace of God, eat of that bread, and drink of that cup.[59]

---

[59] Wesley, *Standard Sermons*, I, 253

Pastor bill said, "When I first came to this church attendance on Communion Sundays was always less than other Sundays. However, that was when we had communion only on the first Sunday of the month. Our church culture has embraced the Lord's Supper weekly, as an indispensable means of grace whereby God blesses us.

So prayer is a means of grace and through prayer and the other means of grace we can support and uplift the ministries of our church.

B. Presence

Pastor Bill then said they would discuss the second thing they should do as members of the Church and this is we should support the church by our presence.

To support the church by our presence naturally means to be present in the services of worship. You are joining the church, you are Christ's, you belong to him, and you are a part of those who give Him their allegiance. Not only should you attend the services; you should want to attend the services to be with God because out of his mercy. He has called you to love him and to be a part of the Church of Christ which loves him.

If you love somebody and they love you, both of you will find ways to be together as often as you can. You have joy in one another and cannot be kept apart. At every opportunity you will try to see the beloved.

This sort of relationship should exist between you and God. Church services and activities are not the only place we can be with him. We just discussed prayer and we do meet him there. We can receive, share in, and share with others this love when we are present in the worship and activities of the church.

This does not mean you have to be a part of every activity within the church. There are limits to your time and your interest, but you should be able to find and participate in those activities of interest to you and to which you can contribute.

Presence means more than just a physical presence. We all know the feeling of being somewhere but with our minds somewhere else; obviously we are not really present. To be present is to be aware, to be aware of what God is saying to us and what we are saying to him in our group worship of Him.

Will your mind wander as it does in prayer? Everybody's mind wanders in prayer. Undoubtedly it will but you are in church for a serious but joyful enjoyment of fellowshipping with God and other who are also worshipping and fellowshipping with you.

If you indeed believe Christ died for you because God loved you, you should want to be in his presence with others who also believe the same things.

C. Gifts

When we speak of gifts and giving gifts to the church we are talking about money, but we are talking about much more than money and something which is vastly more significant and important than money.

"Wow," exclaimed Todd, "what could be more important than money? You can't live without it no matter how hard you try."

"Yes but there must be other things which are important too," replied Diane and she continued, "some people don't have the resources to give much money, like the widow Jesus said gave more than the others. There are other ways we can give also. What about the United Methodist Women and all of the work they do? I know they collect and have money but they do a lot of volunteer work also."

Pastor Bill said, "Let's tackle this problem in two ways. First we will talk about money and then we will talk about other ways to give."

It is easy to say and to see around us the uses of money. We see people who short their families because they are so dedicated to making money. We also see people who do bad or evil things in an effort to get ahead of somebody else. We could give other examples but I think you get the idea.

It is not money itself which is evil. We all need money to purchase our food, clothing, and shelter. Our heavenly Father knows these things. It is when we turn from using money as a necessity to loving money or making money a god we get in trouble with God. You see, when we love money or things money can buy we have changed from loving the creator God to loving something else and the things of this world. There are a lot of nice and pretty things in this world but if we love these creations and not the Creator, we change our relationship with God, making him secondary and worshipping money as our god, our idol. It is this love of money and not God which gets us into trouble, not the use of money.

Money can be used for good but it can also be used for ill. It is not money as such which is to blame but those who use it. In the present state or condition of humanity, money can be an excellent gift of God. In the hands of God's children money can be food for the hungry, drink for the thirsty, and clothes for those who need them. It also gives shelter to those who need it. We can supply the needs of the widow and of the orphan. We may supply a defense for the oppressed, a means of health for the sick, of easing those who are in pain, eyes to the blind, and feet for the lame.

It is therefore important for those who love God to learn how to use this powerful talent or money so we may indeed be faithful stewards of God's grace.

Wesley tried to help us see it correctly in one of his sermons.

The first thing Wesley says we should do is to earn all we can. Here he says and the world understands him at this point and they are together pretty well. There are some conditions though which Wesley puts upon earning money. We should earn all we can without hurting our bodies. We should not work so as to deprive us of the needs of food and sleep which our bodies need. Some employment should be avoided such as those which may be hurtful or unhealthy.

We should gain all we can without hurting our minds. Our minds need to be kept healthy as well as our bodies. So any work which is sinful should be avoided. Anything which robs or defrauds another should likewise to be avoided. Obviously, in the pursuit of money we should not lose our souls. This would not make sense.

Another thing to keep in mind when we are interested in making money is to gain all we can without hurting others. How in the world could we do such a thing, how is it even possible? Wesley provides an answer which though set in a rural community of his time can be understood and adapted to today.

> We cannot, consistent with brotherly love, sell our goods below the market price; we cannot study to ruin our neighbour's trade, in order to advance our own; much less can we entice away, or receive, any of his servants or workmen whom he has need of. None can gain by swallowing up his neighbour's substance, without gaining the damnation of hell![60]

If we do such things today we are hurting others in their substance or right to gain their money.

We should not seek to earn all we can by hurting others physically. In this way we could not sell drugs which hurt others. We cannot play with the lives of others to their detriment. Such an example would be a physician who prolongs a life of pain and disease for the purpose of gaining money rather than helping the patient. We all recognize these extremes.

Neither should we earn our money by hurting others in their soul. If what you do profits the souls of others you are fine but if they are evil in themselves or naturally create evil you cannot do them.

Prostitution thereby is ruled out as an occupation, gambling can be questioned, along with other jobs which individuals will have to work out for themselves. The encouraging of your neighbors to do things which instead of being profitable are harmful or are known to be potentially harmful should be avoided.

Therefore to gain all you can by honest industry is good and fine.

The second thing Wesley says we should do is to save all we can. With this admonition we have dropped some of those who agreed with earning all you can. Not all of those who were with us at the start will leave us at this point, however.

The idea is not to fritter away our earnings. Really we don't need dozens of shoes, coats, trousers etc. We also don't need to eat until we just can't eat anymore and then eat some more until we become much heavier than we should be.

Wesley would have us watch our expenses and be careful to purchase only those things necessary. We do not need to purchase so we may gain the admiration and praise of other humans. Purchase and be content not with the praises of other humans but from God.

The more we purchase to gratify our desires the more our desires outstrip whatever monies we have to purchase. The stronger your attachment to these desires the weaker your desire for God. Your desires can get in the way of your life with God and can begin to take his place in your heart.

---

[60] Wesley, *Standard Sermons*, 2:317

We know none of these things are bad in themselves. The problem is they can easily become more important in our lives than God and then they become idols and we worship not God but non-gods.

If we stop at this point, earning and saving, we will have missed the entire point of Wesley's. Because we do the first two it leads to the real point which is to then *give all we can.*

We should provide for our self and our families—food, clothing, shelter—all these are required for our health and our heavenly Father knows we have need of them. This includes some savings for emergencies and retirement, however with what is left over as you have opportunity, to do good to all men.

As a steward of God's goods before expending money on self or family you can ask yourself if you are acting as a good steward. Are you following God's word? Is this a sacrifice, this expense, one that can be given to Christ? Will this expense help my reward in heaven or hinder it?

Wesley says it so well:

> Our kingdom, our wisdom, is not of this world: heathen custom is nothing to us. We follow no men any farther than they are followers of Christ. Hear ye Him: yea, to-day, while it is called to-day, hear and obey His voice! At this hour, and from this hour, do his will: fulfil His word, in this and in all things! I entreat you, in the name of the Lord Jesus, act up to the dignity of your calling! No more sloth! Whatsoever your hand findeth to do, do it with your might! No more waste! Cut off every expense which fashion, caprice, or flesh and blood demand! No more covetousness! But employ whatever God has entrusted you with, in doing good, all possible good, in every possible kind and degree, to the household of faith, to all men! This is no small part of 'the wisdom of the just.' Give all ye have, as well as all ye

are, a spiritual sacrifice to Him who withheld not from you His Son, His only Son: so 'laying up in store for yourselves a good foundation against the time to come, that ye may attain eternal life'![61]

Pastor Bill said, "It took me a long time to tithe but I finally made it. I was scared I would not have enough left at the end of the month if I gave a tithe but I was able to. One thing it did for me was to make me more aware of my expenses and purchases and defining those which were necessary as opposed to those which were just nice to have. Once you begin to consider it this way there is no need to have the latest and greatest gadget somebody else has. I am able to get my work done effectively with what I have."

"I heard a story of a man who has a Ford and who would ask someone with a very expensive car how much they had paid and he said he paid much less but got to the same meeting. He really caused upsets because he would also ask somebody with an expensive watch what time it was and when they told him he would say, that's great the same time as my Timex from Wal-Mart says."

"I do know of a family who said they were struggling with their company until they decided to tithe. They said after they decided to tithe, their business took off. I dare not say doing the same thing will bring about the same results to anybody else but they swear this is what happened to them."

---

[61] Wesley, *Standard Sermons*, 2, 326-7

D. Service
> Then the king will say to those at his right hand, 'Come, you that are blessed by my Father, inherit the kingdom prepared for you from the foundation of the world; for I was hungry and you game me food, I was thirsty and you gave me something to drink, I was a stranger and you welcomed me, I was naked and you gave me clothing, I was sick and you took care of me, I was in prison and you visited me.' Then the righteous will answer him, 'Lord, when was it that we saw you hungry and gave you food, or thirsty and gave you something to drink? And when was it that we saw you sick or in prison and visited you? And the king will answer them, 'Truly I tell you, just as you did it to one of the least of these who are members of my family, you did it to me.' Matthew 25:34-40

But finances are not the only thing covered when we talk about supporting the church with our gifts. There are gifts of our time and our talents also, which may be called gifts of service.

God has given us all gifts and thank goodness we all have different gifts. In several places Paul talks about these differing gifts and how they all work together for the good of the church community.

They are gifts from God which we have and as good stewards these gifts can be used to uphold the fellowship of the church.

We all are not meant to be ministers. We all are not meant to be prophets. We all cannot teach or lead but what talents we do have can be used to further the cause of God. It takes all the various talents working together to work for God.

Paul tells us these gifts used for God are somewhat like the body. We couldn't live if we were just an eye, or a leg, or a hand, or a nose. All parts of the body are necessary to sustain life and are important just as all gifts are important and can work together. Leading is not better than following, teaching is not better than prophesy, ministering is not better than singing etc… They are all important and they all work together.

Time is another gift we all have. We promise to give our time to the church. We do not promise to give 40 or any amount of hours to the church but those hours left over from earning our living and taking care of our families can be given. If there is no time left for the church we are looking at it incorrectly. God has created us and given us time and as good stewards of this gift some should joyfully be given back to him.

It is hard to understand how someone can love God and the wonderful gifts he has given us without joyfully giving some of our time, talents and money back to him.

E. Witness

After the resurrection Jesus spoke to his disciples.

> And Jesus came and said to them, "All authority in heaven and on earth has been given to me. Go therefore and make disciples of all nations, baptizing them in the name of the Father and of the Son, and of the Holy Spirit, and teaching them to obey everything that I have commanded you. And remember, I am with you always, to the end of the age." Matthew 28:18-20

We are called to be witnesses for Christ. We cannot all preach, but we can share the Word of God, the good news, with others.

Not everyone is called to be a missionary, to go abroad to spread the word of God but we can live our lives as examples of how God has worked and is working in our lives.

Sharing God's love is witnessing to the world. Some can do this by teaching classes or Sunday School or other areas of Christian thought.

Some are able to share God's love by helping the elderly, the young, the sick, or others who are in need of help.

There are an abundance of areas in which we are able to witness to God's love.

"I'm happy but sorry our study is over," said Barb. "I have enjoyed it and each of you. We need to think of what we can do together in the future."

Felista spoke up, "Girls, I'm going to miss you and our time together. I get to talk about something other than lawyer stuff."

"Yeah, where am I going to get coffee, cupcakes and good discussion in the future," said Todd.

"I really won't miss the studying," replied Shawn, "but I will miss you guys and the animated discussions we have had."

"I'd like to thank Pastor Bill for his fine presentations" said Melinda

Barb said, "Pastor Bill will you end our session with a prayer?"

"I'd be happy to," said Pastor Bill. "Let us pray."

On Palm Sunday morning Glenda was baptized.

On Easter Sunday morning Barb and Jim, Shawn and Diane, Todd and Melinda, Felista and James joined St. Mark United Methodist Church and were greeted by the congregation.

SCRIPTURE

But be doers of the word, and not merely hearers who deceive themselves. For if any are hearers of the word and not doers, they are like those who look at themselves in a mirror; for they look at themselves and, on going away, immediately forget what they were like. But those who look into the perfect law, the Law of liberty, and persevere, being not hearers who forget but doers who act—they will be blessed in their doing.

If anyone think they are religious, and do not bridle their tongues but deceive their hearts, their religion is worthless. Religion that is pure and undefiled before God, the Father, is this: to care for orphans and widows in their distress, and to keep oneself unstained by the world.

(James 1:22-27)

PRAYER

O God our Father, lover of all, dispenser of justice, mercy, joy and giver of all graces to us, we thank you for your Son Jesus our Christ, who is our Lord and Savior.

We have now finished this search for knowledge and faith through our studies and work together and we thank you for seeing us through them. We thank you for the members of our study group and for their sharing with the rest of us their thoughts and ideas. We appreciate each of them and each of their contributions to our study.

Be with us in our continued walk with you we ask it in the name of Jesus Christ. Amen.

CHAPTER 10. QUESTIONS

1. Is it important to pray for the ongoing work of our church as well as the special activities of our church? Why?

2. Are we bad Christians if our mind wanders sometimes when we are praying to God?

3. Other than prayer what are other means of grace through which God can reveal himself to us?

4. To be present in church—what does this statement mean? Do we have to be present at all meetings and all services? When should I want to be present?

5. What do we mean by supporting the church with our gifts?

6. What three things did Wesley tell us to do with our money? How does that fit with your experience today?

7. What does it mean by give service to the church?

ANSWERS TO QUESTIONS

Introduction

1. They had not been in church for a long time and had organized their life without church being a part of their life. When the discussion came up they had to consider giving up some things they enjoyed. Jim had a job and therefore had a group of friends readymade but Barb did not. They also enjoyed Sunday breakfasts and when Jim worked around the house on Saturday's, Sunday's were his only time off. He also played golf on some Sundays. Yet as parents they wanted the best for their children and in their case that might mean some sacrifices in order to attain the goal.

2. Definitely in their case the location of the church was a factor. The church was close to where they lived. We don't know if one of them had been a United Methodist, this information was not given yet. However, as members of two different Protestant churches they apparently were not going to a non-protestant church, so they looked at one close by. Their initial inspection of the church did not turn them off—the church grounds were well maintained and there was plenty of parking spaces.

Then when they visited the church they were greeted by members of the congregation. The church bulletin told them there were classes for their child and there were plenty of activities for them to engage in if they desired. They also received a short phone call from the church during the week expressing the church's welcoming them.

3. Pastor Bill was able to see them during the week. After a greeting with coffee and a chat, he lead them through the facility, explaining the function of each building. He listened to them to find out their background and what they were looking for in a church experience. Not always would a pastor be able to take as much time as Pastor Bill did but they were fortunate he was able to make time for them.

Also, it was fortunate he had a membership class starting in a few weeks where they could meet with others who were seeking some of the same things.

4. Jim and Barb did more of a search than many people would. They made a trip to the church to see if it seemed good to them. Others may not have used the phone book; they may have asked friends or just driven around. Different people seek out churches in different ways.

5. Pastor Bill made them welcome, helped them become familiar with the church buildings and the programs currently in the church. Pastor Bill probably overcame their natural hesitancy and helped them look forward to the class.

Chapter 1

1. Some of the organizations discussed were the Sunday School which provides Christian education for people of all ages, from children to adults. The United Methodist Women or UMW was organized for women. They had smaller groups and did a lot of work for missions as well as other activities for women and children. The United Methodist Men, UMM, was organized for men and they met often for coffee or breakfast and they helped around the church to maintain the facility. There were areas of service as well as a Food Pantry and "glazed grace" ministry.

2. The phases of worship presented by Pastor Bill are adoration, confession, illumination, and dedication. Each phase brings a little different direction or focus for the worship experience. There are other ways to look at worship but Pastor Bill has chosen this one which works for him.

3. The church year when followed makes a great deal of sense and it also provides a rounded look at activities and thinking for the entire year—obviously the church year is built around the two great events, which are the birth of Jesus and his death and resurrection. The colors of the church year, when known and followed provide additional worship depth for Christians.

4. All local churches belong to a District. A District can do things which no single church can, such as training, guest speakers, and D.S.'s who work closely with churches and pastors. The District has many of the same committees or positions found in the local churches.

5. District Superintendents or D.S.'s work with pastors to help them be successful. They counsel, train, and meet with pastors to be available for help. The D.S. also has different district committees for the district and leads them. The D.S. also works with the Bishop and other D.S.'s in the Bishop's area to worshipfully try to get the right pastor to the right church. Every United Methodist Church pastor is sent to their charge one year at a time so this work has to be done every year.

6. The Book of Discipline or Discipline gives the rules and organizations the United Methodist Churches are to follow. When there are questions about organizations, relationships between various

parts of the church, membership must belong to various committees etc…the Discipline is a helpful guide.

Chapter 2

1. The Annual Conference has three possible meanings. The first is as the basic unit of the UMC. The Annual Conference is composed of the districts within the Annual Conference, presided over by a Bishop. We could also mean the organization or the professional staff which conducts the ministry and affairs of the Annual Conference. The third usage of the term means the annual meetings of the Annual Conference.

2. Since the meetings are open, anyone can attend who wants to go. Voting is another matter. The Discipline and Annual Conference determine if all ministers can vote or not. Some ministers are just beginning their studies and may or may not be able to vote. The lay delegates elected by their churches are also able to vote. The Discipline also provides for people holding certain jobs within the church to vote.

3. The Annual Conference provides worship services, handles the placement of ministers and their various plans such as health, retirement etc… There are reports from the various boards and agencies as well.

4. The General Conference meets every four years and performs the legislative function of the UMC. The Jurisdictional Conference meets every four years, after the General and it naturally is smaller than the General Conference. The General Conference has members from the entire church whereas the Jurisdictional has only those from one of the 5 jurisdictions.

5. There are several Boards and Commissions in the United Methodist Church, and they are found on several pages in this chapter.

Chapter 3

1. Christianity comes from Judaism. Our history before Christ is the same. Jesus, his disciples and early followers were all Jews. The Jewish Scriptures are our Scriptures as well.

2. Early Christians were probably considered by many Jews as well as others outside Judaism as a sect of Judaism It was only later when the complete break came between the two and Christianity became a separate religion based on the life, teachings, and death of Jesus our Christ.

3. The church used councils in which Christians got together and discussed various issues that had arisen. They usually came to a consensus about one or more topics. In between there were many writings by the Christian leaders explaining the gospel and discussing various concepts.

4. The first Ecumenical Council was held in Nicea in 325 C.E. The council decided that Jesus was fully divine and he was of the same substance as the Father. The second Ecumenical council in Constantinople in 381 C.E. decided the Holy Spirit was likewise of the same substance as the Father and the Son and was not subordinate to either of them. The third was in Chalcedon in 421 C.E. and it determined Jesus was wholly human and wholly divine.

5. The Protestant Reformation began in the 16th century. These churches broke with Rome and rejected the Pope as having authority over them.

6. John Calvin wrote the "Institutes of the Christian Religion," one of the most famous books written about the Christian Religion. He also tried to manage Geneva as a Christian State and founded the Reformed movement. Huldreich Zwingli, and Philip Melanchthon are two more famous names. Martin Luther was the one who kicked it off by nailing his 95 theses on the church door in Wittenberg. He also wrote many books about Christian thought and was the founder of the Lutheran Church. Luther was in Germany or what we call Germany today.

7. John and Charles Wesley did not want to start a new church. What they wanted to do was to provide a leaven or yeast in the Church of

England. In fact they both remained ministers in the Church of England until their death.

8. John allowed laymen to preach the gospel in circuits when he could no longer handle the load. Charles had gotten married by then, had children, and focused on churches around where he lived.

9. We were first The Methodist Episcopal Church at Lovely Lane Chapel in 1784. Two Wesleyan churches were also formed about then. They are, The Church of the United Brethren in Christ and the Evangelical Association. Problems of race relations created two African American Churches. Slavery and race relations caused the church to split into The Methodist Episcopal Church and The Methodist Episcopal Church, South. In 1939 and 1968 various Wesleyan Churches united and in 1968 we became the United Methodist Church.

Chapter 4

1. It is hard to explain the Trinity in rational terms. How can a unity of one be three? It is not as if God was first the Father, then the Son and now the Holy Spirit. God has always been all three or a three-one.

2. You could say that you have three round objects in your pocket and they are called by a single name—coins. However, they are also different or have different sizes and values. In some ways this is like God but in others it is not. We know God and the knowledge we now have of him is through the Spirit. But we as Christians believe in Jesus as the Christ, the Son of God the Father. Wesley called him the Three-One God for lack of a better term. We know God in each of these three forms or persons but how this can be defeats our logic.

3. We believe Jesus was wholly God and wholly human. This is what we mean when we talk about the incarnation. He was born a human baby and died on the cross as God's gift of His Son to us.

4. Again we meet the limits of our human reason. We believe Jesus was the Christ, the Son of God, but we also believe he was human like us so he faced temptations, was hungry and thirsty, bled, and died like us. We know him as both and the Church decided this within the first 500 years.

5. There is as much, in fact more, evidence for the existence of Jesus than for many who lived then and indeed many years later. The disciples were not men of letters with the exception of Paul. Most of them could not write but there were many of his followers who could write and they did write the Gospels and letters which are in the New Testament. Unless all of them who lived apart and wrote their works at different times, were all in on the fantasy or conspiracy, and not one of them ever broke ranks and spilled the beans, it is difficult to believe Jesus did not exist.

6. A similar argument may be made for the resurrection. Some believed or wanted others to believe, that Jesus was spirited away by his disciples and they played a hoax on humanity. But in order to believe this you would have to believe all those people who said they saw and

talked to him individually and in groups, were all in on the hoax and none of them ever broke ranks and said it was really a hoax.

7. The Holy Spirit was sent as the counselor and as God with us. He is the breath of God coming into each of us who accept him. The breath of fresh air which cleanses us, recreates us, is with us. The Holy Spirit is our conscience, who loves us and constantly is calling us back to Jesus and through Him, the Father. The Holy Spirit helps us grow in the Christian life.

8. The fruits of the spirit are God's gifts to us through the Holy Spirit. We can see God working through us when we have accepted and asked him to come within us and we begin to see the fruits of love, peace, joy, patience, kindness, goodness, faithfulness, gentleness, and self-control which was not evident before.

9. Unfortunately what the church has called the seven deadly sins have in many places become the normal behavior in our culture. Often these behaviors are recognized and applauded. The seven sins are deadly because they are not the fruits of the Spirit, nor are they from God—they are against his will for us.

Chapter 5

1. The Scriptures tell us sin has invaded all of our institutions and interactions with each other. Society is nothing but a group of people. If each person, and therefore the group, has been infected by sin it is difficult to believe how we can get better without help from God. Though some become Christians and therefore some in society are Christians this fact does not make society get better and better. As individual Christians we can respond to God's grace and therefore grow as God would have it; all growth or even sustaining, comes from the grace of God.

2. God created us to be with him and love him. God does not change his position day-by-day or hour-by-hour. God wants us to love him and follow his desires for us. As such it was not God who separated himself from us but we who separated ourselves from God. God gave us the ability to choose, we were not created as rock or a machine which has no choice. Created to choose, we chose against God for something which at the time seemed to be more attractive so we chose another god. Since we are the one who chooses, to put something else in the place of God, it was we who are responsible for our sinful choices.

3. In many realms of human study and endeavor man has and can make significant progress. However great humanity's learning etc... in the area which is most important, our relationship with God, we can do nothing except accept his grace. This is not to divorce God from all human endeavors because he is working there too, even if we do not see him. Salvation comes from God not from human works, learning, sacrifice, or achievement.

4. Preventing or prevenient grace is God's grace which is given to everyone. This grace allows us to make the choice to accept his grace and respond to His love or to say no to God and turn him down as the most important relationship in our life.

5. There is still sin because we are sinful beings. God may offer salvation but we may not accept it. Even if one accepts God's gift we still may sin. Sometimes the sin is known and sometimes it is not. There are also those who do not accept God's offer and therefore are sinners. Then, there is indeed evil in this world.

6. Prevenient grace is our understanding of God's gift to us of the ability to choose for or against him. Of course he wants everyone in the world to accept Him but He has given us the marvelous power of accepting Him.

7. By this term Wesley means God's prevenient grace is given to us—it does not come to us by anything which we can do. Even our choice for God by his prevenient grace is God's gift not our work. By free in all Wesley means God's prevenient grace is given to all, not just those who respond to him.

Chapter 6

1. Some of the most commonly used bible versions are the King James, New King James, Revised Standard Version and New RSV, and the New International Version. I personally like to compare the NRSV, NIV, and "The Message." They each have a way of speaking to me and I enjoy the turn of phrase in some of them.

2. Student Bibles can give us an abundance of information about the Bible such as the times in which the various books were written, the ideas or experiences behind the writing, i.e. what they were trying to do. Explanations of Jewish poetry have certainly helped me to better understand and appreciate the Psalms and other poetry in the Bible. The geography and history of the Biblical world is also helpful. Other information is provided in various Student Bibles.

3. Our experiences and knowledge may have changed. Weapons of war, money or coins may likewise change as well as clothing, cars, music, medicine and machines. However, in the basic area of sin in our life, nothing has changed. We are all still sinners, we all still need God, and we all need his grace to grow as he would have us grow, in the knowledge and love of him.

4. The Old Testament is our Scripture as well as the New Testament. The history of the Old Testament is our history, the love of God in the Old Testament is the love we enjoy, and the ways to please God in the Old Testament are the same for us. The only difference is in the New Testament the Christ has come, clarified our understanding of God, and made possible the renewed relationship with God that we call salvation.

5. Wesley said we were to read the Scriptures and usually the straight forward meaning was correct but if we were unsure or there were conflicting passages we could look first at the Christian traditions and see what they can provide for us in understanding. The second tool is to read other Scriptures on the same point. The third is to use our best reasoning and the fourth is experience, and here he means our experience with God.

Chapter 7

1. We were created good by God, we were created in his image, we were created to be in relationship and love with him but something happened to separate us. This separation could not and did not come from God. The Bible tells us Adam (humanity) chose against God and not to follow His loving will for us. That disease has gone down through all people through all generations.

2. Justification is God's action on our behalf. The term means our past sins are forgiven. Since everyone needs their sins forgiven everyone needs to be justified. However not everyone will accept God's love and follow him. Some say they do but really don't. They may be part timers who follow sometimes but not always. In truth, they do not really follow Him because those who follow Him have put God at the center of their lives.

3. No, only God is holy and if we are holy it is God's gift to us. He expects us to be holy and wants us to accept the gift of holiness, but we have to open our hearts and lives to accept His holiness.

4. Faith is the only thing necessary for salvation. Faith is not mere belief whereby one says "I believe in God." Faith is a trust and response to God that says "yes" to this relationship.

5. Justification can only take care of past sins. From this point on we can continue in the loving relationship or we can at some point decide not to continue in the saving relationship. God has not made us machines which do not have choices. Our relationship with God is ever dependent upon us accepting God's graces or denying them. God's word is true and we will trust God fully knowing that what he says is true and he will perform and give us the gifts he says he will give.

6. Yes, justified Christians can sin. There are two types of sin which can happen to a justified Christian but one type can hardly be called a sin. That type of sin is due to our imperfect knowledge which, with the bests of intents, can lead to sin such as hurting another unknowingly, etc… The real sin is when we again turn our backs on God and sin again knowingly choosing something other than God for God. In this case we ask forgiveness of God and once more follow his will for us.

7. Christian Perfection has nothing to do with knowing everything there is to know etc…It does not mean we can perfectly see the future. Christian Perfection is to be perfected in the love of God and our fellow humans. The second description is to have the entire mind that was in Christ which lets us walk as Christ walked. The third is purity of intention whereby we dedicate our entire lives to God.

8. They are described above.

9. Yes we can receive God's gift of perfection in this life. However it most frequently is given just before death. There is no reason why God may not give this gift to us now if we earnestly seek after it and pray for it.

Chapter 8

1. When we see someone help another or contribute to a worthy cause, perform an act of heroism, or create something useful for humanity we may say these are good works—and they are good works. The entire world would agree with us here. However to the Christian no work is good unless it is a work performed after the Christian has been justified. Works before justification, in this sense, cannot be called "good." These works are acceptable in the sight of God because they arise out of love for him and following his ways and paths. They come out because of the Christians faith in Jesus.

2. and 3. Good works come after justification and not before to Protestant Christians. Good works such as feeding the poor, helping the widow etc... engaged in before justification are nice but they have nothing to do with the saving relationship with God. Works play no role in the process leading up to justification in the sense they cannot be offered to God as payment for salvation. Justification is the gift of God not the work of humans forcing God's hand. Our Roman Catholic brothers believe good works after justification can be done and are in excess of the good works required by God. The excess of good works can then be applied to others who do not have enough good works. Protestants believe we cannot perform enough good works so there is an excess. Even if we do all good works we still fall short. It is impossible to have good works in excess of fully following the law of God.

4. Baptism and the Lord's Supper. The Roman Catholic Church around 1500 C.E. determined there were seven. In the Protestant Reformation it was decided that there were only two.

5. The matter in baptism is water and the form in baptism is the words of consecration i.e., "I baptize you in the name of the Father, the Son, and the Holy Spirit."

6. Methodists will do all three. We do not find in Scripture a single prescribed method.

7. Baptism initiates us into a covenant or agreement with God just as circumcision did and does for the Jews. Those who were outside the loving relationship with God have become children of God.

8. There is no reason for a second baptism. One baptism is enough whether you were baptized by immersion, pouring or sprinkling does not matter to us.

9. The Lord's Supper should be partaken as frequently as it is offered and you have occasion. This is a sacrament of God and the Lord's Table. It should be partaken of seriously, joyfully, and as frequently as offered. God can and does meet us in this sacrament so we should gladly participate as often as it is offered. Also, it is the command of Christ and the benefits we receive such as forgiveness and nourishing our souls.

10. We should come to the table in the spirit of faith. We are aware of our unworthiness and yet we can trust his promise that he will be present when we receive the elements.

11. Jesus gave the disciples both of them and we see no reason why we should not be given both the wine or grape justice and the bread. Jesus gave his body and blood for us and we can remember him and meet him in both elements.

12. The Supper represents the sufferings of Christ and in this way it is a memorial. Christ is really present in the super and through these elements God gives us his spiritual graces. The Supper also represents our future partaking of the heavenly banquet with Christ.

Chapter 9

1. The church can mean the building or the group of people who worship there. We can also mean a group of churches such as those in a district or Bishop's area or we can mean the entire United Methodist Church or the church universal.

2. Those things they must have in common are one spirit, one hope, one faith, one baptism, and one God and Father of us all.

3. The first is a living faith; the second is the preaching of the Word of God; and the third is the sacraments are duly administered.

4. Protestants do not believe in purgatory like the Roman Catholics. We cannot find it in the Scriptures.

5. If we cannot understand what is being said how can we receive the Word of God?

6. We are not bound to using any specific rites. We are free to choose as long as they are not against the Word of God.

7. We do not have to follow a particular ceremony a particular way as long as it is not against the Word of God.

8. True religion is a religion of the heart to love God and love our neighbor.

Chapter 10

1. Prayer supports all the ministries of the church. Without prayer we would not be able to keep our ministries going.

2. Our minds will wander because we are human. Just go back to talking with God. We are not bad Christians if our minds wander.

3. Two more are reading the Scripture and the Lord's Supper.

4. We should want to attend the worship services and to take advantage of other meetings and activities as we can contribute to and enjoy. Just because we are tired or want to do something else, etc… is not a reason for missing church.

5. Naturally we must support the church with our money. The church cannot survive without money. There are many costs to keep the church open so we can worship.

6. Earn all you can, save all you can, so you can give all you can.

7. Serving the church by using the gifts God has given us and serving our fellow humans the same way.

Bibliography
Primary Sources

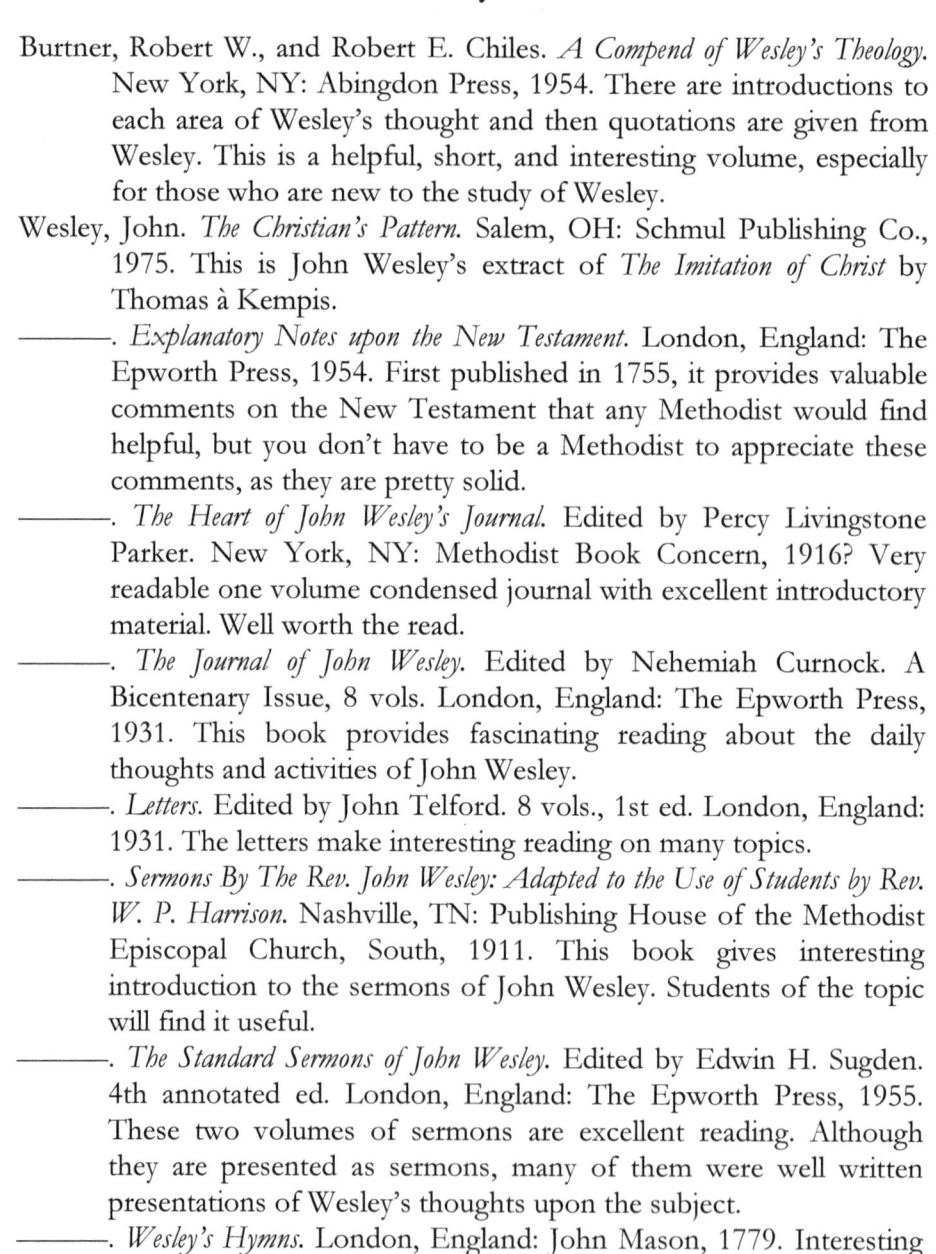

Burtner, Robert W., and Robert E. Chiles. *A Compend of Wesley's Theology.* New York, NY: Abingdon Press, 1954. There are introductions to each area of Wesley's thought and then quotations are given from Wesley. This is a helpful, short, and interesting volume, especially for those who are new to the study of Wesley.

Wesley, John. *The Christian's Pattern.* Salem, OH: Schmul Publishing Co., 1975. This is John Wesley's extract of *The Imitation of Christ* by Thomas à Kempis.

———. *Explanatory Notes upon the New Testament.* London, England: The Epworth Press, 1954. First published in 1755, it provides valuable comments on the New Testament that any Methodist would find helpful, but you don't have to be a Methodist to appreciate these comments, as they are pretty solid.

———. *The Heart of John Wesley's Journal.* Edited by Percy Livingstone Parker. New York, NY: Methodist Book Concern, 1916? Very readable one volume condensed journal with excellent introductory material. Well worth the read.

———. *The Journal of John Wesley.* Edited by Nehemiah Curnock. A Bicentenary Issue, 8 vols. London, England: The Epworth Press, 1931. This book provides fascinating reading about the daily thoughts and activities of John Wesley.

———. *Letters.* Edited by John Telford. 8 vols., 1st ed. London, England: 1931. The letters make interesting reading on many topics.

———. *Sermons By The Rev. John Wesley: Adapted to the Use of Students by Rev. W. P. Harrison.* Nashville, TN: Publishing House of the Methodist Episcopal Church, South, 1911. This book gives interesting introduction to the sermons of John Wesley. Students of the topic will find it useful.

———. *The Standard Sermons of John Wesley.* Edited by Edwin H. Sugden. 4th annotated ed. London, England: The Epworth Press, 1955. These two volumes of sermons are excellent reading. Although they are presented as sermons, many of them were well written presentations of Wesley's thoughts upon the subject.

———. *Wesley's Hymns.* London, England: John Mason, 1779. Interesting reading for the various hymns topics and the poetry of both John and Charles Wesley.

———. *Wesley's Notes on the Bible*. Edited by G. Roger Schoenhals. Grand Rapids, MI: Francis Asbury Press, 1987. Wesley's multi-volume *Notes on the Old Testament* is also available but this is a one volume set which includes portions of Wesley's comments on both the Old and New Testaments.

———. *The Works of John Wesley*. Edited by Thomas Jackson. 14 vols, 3rd ed. Grand Rapids, MI: Zondervan Publishing House, 1958–59. This is the first complete unabridged edition in nearly 100 years reproduced from the 1872 authorized edition and it contains an abundance of John's writings.

Wesley, John, and John Fletcher. *Entire Sanctification: Attainable in this Life*. Salem, OH: Schmul Publishing Co., date unknown. John Fletcher was one of John Wesley's preachers and an excellent theologian in his own right. Even though it is a little difficult to read, this is an interesting publication about Christian perfection. It is one of the most complete statements on Christian perfection that I have read. Paragraphs are numbered and there is a long question and answer section.

Secondary Sources

The Book of Discipline of the United Methodist Church. Nashville, TN: The United Methodist Publishing House, 20412. Any recent *Discipline* will have the theology of the United Methodist Church in them. Disciplines before the Methodist Church became united will also have the same theology that was given to the church by John Wesley.

Baines-Griffiths, David, *Wesley the Anglican*, London, Macmillan and Col, LTD, 1919

Baker, Frank, *John Wesley and the Church of England*, London, Epworth Press, 1970. This is the best book I have read concerning the topic.

Bell, Terry, *The Love Ethic*, Advantage Books, 2008. He does an excellent job in working with the Love Ethic which is Agape.

Berger, Teresa, *Theology in Hymns*, Nashville, Kingswood Books, 1995. A book on the relationship of doxology and theology from the collection of hymns for Methodists.

Bryan, John L., *John Wesley The First Methodist*, Washington D.C., General Board of Temperance of The Methodist Church, 1960. Very short and brief, but interesting.

Cadman, S. Parks, *Three Religious Leaders of Oxford*, New York, Macmillan, 1918

Calvin, John, *Calvin's Institutes*, Grand Rapids, Michigan, Wm. B. Eerdmans Publishing Company, 1957. This is an excellent rendition of the Institutes of John Calvin, translated by Henry Beveridge.

_____, *A Compend of the Institutes of the Christian Religion*, ed. Hugh Thomson Kerr, Jr., Philadelphia, Presbyterian Board of Christian Education, 1939. This is a helpful book for one trying to get into the theology of John Calvin.

Cannon, William R. *The Theology of John Wesley*. New York, NY: Abingdon Press, 1946. Dr. Cannon gives a very capable and readable theology of John Wesley.

Chappell, E. B., *Studies in the Life of John Wesley*, Nashville, Publishing House, M.E. Church, South, 1914

Chilcote, Paul W., ed. *Wesleyan Tradition: a Paradigm for Renewal*. Nashville, TN: Abingdon Press, 2002. This is a good book, containing worthwhile material, but is not for the timid reader.

_____, *Recapturing the Wesley's' Vision*, Downers Grove, Illinois, IVP Academic, 2004. A must book for the serious student of Wesley which presents his both/and elements.

Clark, Dougan, *The Theology of Holiness*, Schmul, 1996

Collins, Kenneth J., and John H. Tyson. *Conversion in the Wesleyan Tradition*. Nashville, TN: Abingdon Press, 2001. This is an interesting book, but difficult for the average layperson to read.

_____, *The Scripture Way of Salvation*, Nashville, Abingdon Press, 1997. This is a necessary book for the serious student of Wesley. Accounts for the dynamic or tension which is present in Wesley's theology.

_____, *A Faithful Witness: John Wesley's Homiletical Theology*, Wilmore, Kentucky, Wesley Heritage Press.

_____, *Power, Politics and the Fragmentation of Evangelicalism*, Downers Grove, Ill, IVP Academic, 2012. An excellent exposition of evangelicalism of the past century, where liberals and conservatives both have gone wrong and the way forward.

_____, *John Wesley: A Theological Journey*, Nashville, Abingdon Press, 2003. Wonderful tracing of Wesley's theological grown through his life.

_____, *Wesley on Salvation: A Study in the Standard Sermons*, Grand Rapids, Francis Asbury Press, 1989, Presents the key theological ideas of Wesley on the doctrine of Salvation.

Daniels, W. H. *The Illustrated History of Methodism in Great Britain and America: From the Days of the Wesleys to the Present Time.* New York, NY: Methodist Book Concern, 1879.

Davey, Cyril. *John Wesley and the Methodists.* Nashville, TN: Abingdon Press, 1985. This is a small book that has lots of excellent pictures. It contains some good information and is very readable.

Eldridge, Charles O. *A Popular Exposition of Methodist Theology.* Salem, OH: Schmul Publishing Co., reprint 1982. Original date unknown. This is a good book that the layperson will find easy to read.

Ewbank, J. Robert, *John Wesley, Natural Man, and the "Isms,"* Eugene, Oregon, Wipf and Stock, 2009. This book discusses Wesley's theological thinking about natural man, heathens, Judaism, deism, Roman Catholicism, Quakerism, and mysticism.

_____. *Wesley's Wars,* Bloomington, Indiana, WestBow Press, 2012. This book discusses the theological battles John Wesley fought to keep his followers free from theological error, particularly original sin, prevenient grace, good works, Christian perfection, the Church of England and the Catholic Church.

Faulkner, John Alfred, *Wesley as Sociologist, Theologian, Churchman,* New York, The Methodist Book Concern, 1918

Felton, Gayle Carlton, *This Holy Mystery,* Nashville, Discipleship Resources, 2005

_____ *United Methodists and the Sacraments,* Nashville, Abingdon Press, 2007

_____ *By Water and the Spirit,* Nashville, Discipleship Resources, reprinted 2014

Fletcher, John, *John Wesley the Methodist: A Plain Account of His Life and Work,* New York, Eaton & Mains, 1903

Fletcher, William H., *Wesley and His Century: A Study in Spiritual Forces,* New York, Eaton & Mains, 1907

Forsyth, P. T. *The Person and Place of Jesus Christ.* Congregational Union Lecture, 1909. London, England: Whales/Hodder & Stoughton, 1909. Forsyth was able to say things in an excellent manner. It is too bad that most of his books are extremely hard to find.

Gooch, John O., *Being a Christian in the Wesleyan Tradition,* Nashville, Discipleship Resources, 2009

_____. *John Wesley for the 21st Century,* Nashville, Discipleship Resources, 2006, an introduction to Methodism for those who sit in Methodist pews but are lacking in this knowledge.

Green, Richard, *The Works of John and Charles Wesley: A Biography,* London, Kelly, 1896

Green, Vivian. *John Wesley and Oxford.* Oxford, England: Thomas-Photos, 1979. A very easy booklet to read, containing many pictures and some information about John when he was at Oxford.

Grudem, Wayne, *Systematic Theology,* Leicester, England, Inter-Varsity Press, 2000. This is an excellent book on systematic theology written from the reformed perspective. The book takes into account other positions as well. A must read for any serious scholar.

Harper, Steve. *John Wesley's Message For Today.* Grand Rapids, MI: Zondervan Publishing House, 1983. This is a very readable, but solid, book for the layperson.

Heitzenrater, Richard P., *The Elusive Mr. Wesley,* 2 vols. Nashville, Abingdon Press, 1984. This is a very able and interesting pursuit of the real John Wesley, not a Wesley written by those who saw no wrong, no error, no problems with his life or thought nor a Wesley who was stuck with one idea. The presentation is of a very complex person.

Harrington, William Holden, *John Wesley, in Company with High Churchmen,* London, Church Press Co., 1869

Hildebrandt, Franz. *Christianity According to the Wesleys.* London, England: The Epworth Press, 1956. These are the Harris Franklin Rall Lectures of 1954 delivered at Garrett Biblical Institute, Evanston, Illinois. This book contains solid material but remains a readable book.

Holmes, David, *The Wesley Offering: or Wesley and His Times,* Boston, James F. Magee, 1860

Hurst, John Fletcher. *The History of Methodism.* 6 vols. New York, NY: Eaton & Mains, 1902. Undoubtedly out of print, but has some good material in it.

Hyde, A. B. *The Story of Methodism.* Greenfield, MA: Willey & Co., 1887. Probably out of print by now but an interesting book for those who like to read the history.

James, William. *The Varieties of Religious Experience: A Study in Human Nature.* New York, NY: Modern Library, 1994. This is a classic that I am glad to say is still around and may be purchased at many bookstores.

Job, Rueben P. *A Wesleyan Spiritual Reader.* Nashville, TN: Abingdon Press, 1998. A Methodist Bishop uses Wesley as a basis for devotional readings. This is a very readable book with lots of good material. The layperson will have no difficulty with this one.

―――. *Three Simple Rules: A Wesleyan Way of Living*. Nashville, TN: Abingdon Press, 2007. Bishop Rueben takes the rules of Wesley and elaborates upon them for the modern reader. This book is worthwhile and is very readable for the layperson.

Kierkegaard, Soren, *The Concept of Dread*, Princeton, Princeton University Press, 1957

Kirlew, Marianne, *The Story of John Wesley*, Norwich, Fletcher & Sons, 1895

Klaiber, Walter, and Manfred Marquardt. *Living Grace: An Outline of United Methodist Theology.* Translated by J. Steven O'Malley and Ulrike R. M. Guthrie. Nashville, TN: Abingdon Press, 2001. Tough sledding to read through this book for a layperson as it is written for those familiar with theology.

Latourette, Kenneth Scott. *A History of Christianity.* New York, NY: Harper & Brothers, 1953. Though a classic and very long, over 1400 pages, it is shorter than many others. Well written.

Lee, Umphrey. *John Wesley and Modern Religion.* Nashville, TN: Cokesbury, 1936. This is a readable book about John Wesley. It is difficult to find but worth the search.

Lindstrom, Harald. *Wesley and Sanctification.* 1950. Reprint, London, England: The Epworth Press, 1956. This is an excellent study on the topic, but perhaps not the easiest for the layperson.

Maddox, Randy L., et al. *Rethinking Wesley's Theology for Contemporary Methodism.* Nashville, TN: Kingswood Books, 1998. Due to the topic it is an interesting book. However it is difficult for the average layperson.

Matthaei, Sondra Higgins, *Making Disciples*, Nashville, Abingdon Press, 2000. A depth study of education in John Wesley's life and since. A good read.

McConnell, Francis J. *John Wesley.* New York, NY: Abingdon Press, 1939. This is a very readable volume about the life of John Wesley and some of his thoughts. Well worth the time an effort to read.

McNeer, May, and Lynd Ward. *John Wesley.* Nashville, TN: Abingdon-Cokesbury Press, 1951. This is a small, very easy to read book that gives some of the history of John.

Meeks, M. Douglas (ed.) *Trinity Community and Power: Mapping trajectories in Wesleyan Theology*, Nashville, Kingswood Books, 2000. This book brings together the thinking of several scholars on the Trinity and our lives. This is an excellent read for the student.

Nagler, Arthur W. *The Church in History.* New York, NY: Abingdon Press, 1929. Worth the read if you can find it.

Neve, J. L. *A History of Christian Thought.* 2 vols. Philadelphia, PA: Muhlenberg Press, 1946. Excellent history that is readable. This book is undoubtedly out of date now.

Norwood, Frederick A. *The Development of Modern Christianity since 1500.* New York, NY: Abingdon Press, 1956. A good, short history that is readable.

Nygren, Anders. *Agape and Eros.* Translated by Philip S. Watson. London, England: S.P.C.K. Press, 1957. An excellent study of these two words which are so basic to Christianity.

Oden, Thomas C., *The Transforming Power of Grace*, Nashville, Abingdon Press, 1993. This is the best exposition of grace that I have ever read. This is a must for anyone interested in the topic.

_____, *the Rebirth of Orthodoxy*, San Francisco, Harper, 2003. This is an important book for Christians to read. It covers the proposed necessity of Orthodoxy and its growing interest by Christians.

_____, *John Wesley's Scriptural Christianity*, Grand Rapids, Zondervan Publishing House, 1994. Oden has done us a real favor by writing this book which presents John Wesley's theology in order, plus showing us which elements of theology Wesley is expositing for each of his sermons.

_____, *Pastoral Theology*, San Francisco, Harper and Row, 1983. This is an excellent book on the theology about the Christian the ministry. It provides a much needed foundation for the understanding of the activities of the minister.

Outler, Albert C. ed, *John Wesley*, New York, Oxford Press, 1964

_____, *Theology in the Wesleyan Spirit*, Nashville, Discipleship Resources, 1975

_____, *John Wesley's Sermons: An Introduction*, Nashville, Abingdon Press, 1991

Perkins, Barbara, et al. *Benet's Reader's Encyclopedia of American Literature.* New York, NY: HarperCollins Publishers, 1991.

Pike, G. Holden, *John Wesley: The Man and His Mission*, London, The Religious Tract Society, 1904

Pollock, John. *John Wesley.* Wheaton, IL: Victor Books, 1989. This is a very readable and interesting book, mainly about Wesley's life.

Potts, James H., *The Living Thoughts of John Wesley*, New York, Eaton & Mains, 1891

Powell, Samuel M., *A Theology of Christian Spirituality*, Nashville, Abingdon Press, 2005. Gives historical to modern ideas of the necessity of

Rattenbury, J. Ernest. *The Eucharistic Hymns of John and Charles Wesley.* London, England: The Epworth Press, 1948. This is a very able presentation for those interested in the hymns of the Wesley's, particularly those about Holy Communion.

———. *The Evangelical Doctrines of Charles Wesley's Hymns.* 3rd ed. London, England: The Epworth Press, 1954. An excellent work on the doctrines found within the Wesleyan hymns.

———. *Wesley's Legacy to the World.* London, England: The Epworth Press, 1938. Well done and very organized approach to the topics. It is a readable book for the non scholar.

Reed, Bishop Marshall R., *Achieving Christian Perfection*, Nashville, Methodist Evangelistic Materials, 1962. This is a short book for laypersons on modern thoughts on Christian Perfection. It is unfortunately not nearly as deep as Wesley, but provides some interesting thoughts.

Rupp, E. Gordon and Watson, Philip S., *Luther and Erasmus: Free Will and Salvation*, Philadelphia, Westminster Press, 1969. Thoughtfully and well done translations of the differences between Luther and Erasmus on this point.

Runyon, Theodore, *The New Creation*, Nashville, Abingdon Press, 1998

Russell, Cherman Apt, *Standing in the Light*, New York, Basic Books, 2008

Simon, John S., *John Wesley and the Religious Societies*, London, Epworth Press, 1925

Todd, John M. *John Wesley and the Catholic Church.* London, England: Hodder and Stoughton, 1958. Written by a Catholic, it is an interesting interpretation of John Wesley. Shows how Wesley can be used for the ecumenical work of the church.

The United Methodist Hymnal. Nashville, TN: The United Methodist Publishing House, 1992. Other hymn books have replaced this one.

Tyerman, L., *The Life and Times of the Rev. John Wesley*, M.A., 3 vols, New York, Burt Franklin, 1872. This is an old standard, but modern research has made it somewhat outdated.

Tyson, John R. *Assist Me to Proclaim*, Grand Rapids, William B. Eerdmans Publishing Company, 2007. A wonderful presentation of Charles Wesley's hymns and his relationship with John, as well as how some of the hymns portray their theological and daily problems.

Vickers, Jason E., *Wesley: A Guide for the Perplexed*, New York, T & T Clark International, 2009. This is a clear and concise explanation of Wesley's theology as you will find.

Watkins, W. T. *Out of Aldersgate*. Nashville, TN: Dept. of Education and Promotion, Board of Missions, Methodist Episcopal Church, South, 1937. A good, interesting, if somewhat outdated read.

Watson, Philip S. *The Message of the Wesleys*. Grand Rapids, MI: Zondervan Publishing House, 1984. Has introductory comments by Watson and then quotes Wesley. A good read for the interested layperson.

Watson, Richard. *The Life of the Rev. John Wesley*. Translated and noted by John Emory. New York, NY: B. Waugh & T. Mason, 1832. This obviously is an old book, probably out of print, but it is very readable and well worth the time needed to read it.

Weems, Lovett H. Jr., *John Wesley's Message Today*, Nashville, Abingdon Press, 1982. This Pocket Guide book may be small but it contains a good, solid theological background for the layperson.

Wellman, Sam. *John Wesley, Founder of the Methodist Church*. Uhrichsville, OH: Barbour Publishing Inc., 1997. This book is extremely readable; covers mainly his life but not much of his thought.

The Wesley Orders of Common Prayer. Edited by Edward C. Hobbs. Nashville, TN: Board of Education of the Methodist Church: 1957. This is a useful book for the layperson.

Whedon, Daniel A., *John Wesley's View of Entire Sanctification*, *Wesleyan Methodist Magazine* 85 (1862):1015-20; 1090—93

Williams, Colin W. *John Wesley's Theology Today*. New York, NY: Abingdon Press, 1955. A must read book for one seeking to understand the order of salvation by Wesley. It is also written with an eye to the ecumenical movement.

Wood, Allan W. "Deism." In *Encyclopedia of Religion*, 2nd ed., 2251. Detroit, MI: Macmillan, 2005.

Yrigoyen, Charles Jr., *John Wesley: Holiness of Heart & Life*, Nashville, Abingdon Press, 1996. This is a must book for anyone seriously studying the full Christian life.